GUIDE TO DEEPSEEK FOR BEGINNERS

Effortlessly 10x Your Productivity,
Build And Monetize AI Agents, With
600+ Prompts And 50 Business Ideas

By

Nick Droom

Table of Contents

Introduction

Welcome to **Guide to DeepSeek for Beginners: Effortlessly 10x Your Productivity, Build and Monetize AI Agents, With 600+ Prompts and 50 Business Ideas**. If you're holding this book, chances are you've heard the buzz about artificial intelligence transforming how we work, create, and even earn a living. Maybe you're curious, maybe you're skeptical, or maybe you're just tired of slogging through repetitive tasks and wondering if there's a better way. Whatever brought you here, I'm glad you made it. This book is your practical, no-nonsense companion to mastering DeepSeek—a tool that's shaking up how beginners and pros alike approach productivity and innovation.

I wrote this book because I've been where you are. A few years back, I was juggling a full-time job, a side hustle, and a personal life that felt like it was slipping through my fingers. My inbox was a nightmare, my to-do list never shrank, and every day felt like a race against the clock. Then I stumbled across AI tools—DeepSeek among them—and everything changed. It wasn't instant magic, mind you. I had to figure things out through trial and error, piecing together what worked from scattered blog posts, forums, and my own experiments. What I found was a way to cut my workload in half, build systems that ran themselves, and even turn my tinkering into a small income stream. This book is the guide I wish I'd had back then—clear, actionable, and packed with everything a beginner needs to hit the ground running.

Let's get one thing straight: this isn't about turning you into a tech wizard overnight. You don't need to know how to code, understand algorithms, or have a degree in computer science. DeepSeek is built for people like us—regular folks who want results without drowning in jargon or complexity. Whether you're a freelancer trying to manage clients, a small business owner looking to save time, or someone with a spark of an idea they want to turn into cash, this book will show you how to make DeepSeek work for you. By the end, you'll have the tools to boost your output tenfold, create AI agents that handle tasks on autopilot, and even explore ways to make money with what you build.

So, what's DeepSeek? At its core, it's an AI platform that lets you automate tasks, generate ideas, and solve problems faster than you ever thought possible. Think of it like a super-smart assistant who's always ready to help—except it doesn't need coffee breaks or a paycheck. From drafting emails to brainstorming business plans, DeepSeek takes the heavy lifting off your shoulders. But it's more than just a time-saver. It's a gateway to creating what I call "AI agents"—customized helpers you design to tackle specific jobs. And once you've got those agents humming along, you can start thinking about how to share them with others for profit. That's the beauty of this tool: it scales with you, from personal productivity to entrepreneurial possibilities.

This book is broken into seven chapters, each one building on the last to give you a complete roadmap. We'll start with the basics—how to set up DeepSeek and get comfortable using it. Then we'll move into practical ways to slash your workload and free up your time. After that, I'll walk you through building your first AI agent, step by step, so you can see how easy it is to put this tech to work. From there, we'll explore how to turn those agents into money-makers, with real-world examples and 50 business ideas you can adapt to your own goals. Along the way, I've included over 600 prompts—specific instructions you can feed into DeepSeek to get exactly what you need, whether it's a blog post, a marketing plan, or a troubleshooting fix. These prompts are battle-tested; I've used them myself, and they'll save you hours of guesswork.

One thing I want to emphasize: this isn't about replacing you. There's a lot of noise out there about AI taking jobs or making humans obsolete. I don't buy it. DeepSeek isn't here to steal your thunder—it's here to amplify it. You're still the one steering the ship, setting the goals, and making the decisions. What this tool does is clear the deck so you can focus on what matters. For me, that meant more time with my family and less time staring at spreadsheets. For you, it might mean launching that project you've been dreaming about or finally getting ahead of your workload. Whatever your "why," DeepSeek can help you get there.

Now, let's talk about who this book is for. If you're brand new to AI, perfect—this is your starting line. If you've dabbled in other tools but haven't tried DeepSeek yet, you'll find plenty here to make the switch worthwhile. Even if you're just curious about what all the AI fuss is about, stick around; I promise you'll walk away with something useful. The only requirement is a willingness to try something new. You don't need a big budget or fancy equipment—just a computer, an internet connection, and an open mind.

I've tried to keep this book as hands-on as possible. Every chapter includes examples, tips, and prompts you can use right away. I'm not here to bore you with theory or overhype the tech with pie-in-the-sky promises. My goal is to give you practical steps that deliver results. When I first started with DeepSeek, I was amazed at how quickly I could go from "I have no idea what I'm doing" to "Hey, this actually works!" That's the experience I want for you. And if you hit a snag—say, a setting doesn't make sense or an agent isn't behaving—there's a troubleshooting section to get you back on track.

A quick word on the prompts: they're the heart of this book. I've spent months refining them, testing what gets the best output from DeepSeek. You'll find prompts for everything—organizing your schedule, writing sales copy, even generating creative ideas when you're stuck. They're written in plain English, so you can copy them, tweak them, or use them as inspiration. The 50 business ideas, meanwhile, are a mix of things I've seen work and concepts I've brainstormed myself. Some are simple, like selling custom AI agents to local businesses; others are more ambitious, like launching an online service powered by DeepSeek. Pick what fits your skills and interests, and run with it.

One of the best parts about DeepSeek is how it grows with you. Start small—maybe you just want to automate your grocery list or draft emails faster. As you get the hang of it, you can build agents to handle bigger tasks, like managing social media or analyzing data. And if you're feeling entrepreneurial, you can take those skills to market. I've seen people use tools like this to launch side hustles, impress their bosses, or even pivot to entirely new careers. The limit isn't the tech—it's your imagination.

Before we jump in, let me share a quick story. Last year, a friend of mine—let's call her Sarah—was drowning in her freelance graphic design business. She loved the creative side but hated the admin work: invoicing, client follow-ups, scheduling. I showed her DeepSeek, and within a week, she'd built an agent to handle all of that. Not only did she save 10 hours a week, but she started offering "automation packages" to her clients, charging a tidy fee to set up similar systems for them. Now she's got a whole new revenue stream, and she's happier than ever. That's the kind of shift I want you to experience—less grind, more freedom.

This book isn't about perfection. You'll make mistakes, and that's fine. I did too—like the time I built an agent to write blog posts and ended up with 500 words of gibberish because I wasn't specific enough. Laugh it off, adjust, and keep going. DeepSeek is forgiving, and the more you play with it, the better you'll get. My hope is that by the time you finish these pages, you'll feel confident, excited, and ready to make this tool your own.

So, grab a coffee, flip to Chapter 1, and let's get started. You're about to discover how a little AI can go a long way—and I'm here to guide you every step of the journey. Let's do this.

Chapter 1

Introduction to DeepSeek and AI Productivity

Welcome to the first step of your journey with DeepSeek. If you're new to artificial intelligence or just curious about what this tool can do, you're in the right place. This chapter is all about laying the groundwork—helping you understand what DeepSeek is, why it matters, and how it can change the way you work. I remember when I first heard about AI tools like this; I was equal parts excited and overwhelmed, wondering if they were too complicated for someone like me. Spoiler: they're not. My goal here is to make things clear, practical, and maybe even a little fun.

We'll cover what makes DeepSeek special, why AI agents are becoming a big deal, how this tool can supercharge your productivity, and what you should expect as a beginner. By the end, you'll have a solid foundation to start exploring DeepSeek with confidence. Let's get to it.

What is DeepSeek?

DeepSeek is a powerful AI platform designed to help you work smarter, not harder. Imagine having a tireless assistant who can write emails, brainstorm ideas, analyze data, or automate repetitive tasks—all in seconds. That's DeepSeek in a nutshell. It's built to take complex technology and make it accessible, so you don't need to be a programmer or tech guru to use it. Whether you're a student, a freelancer, a small business owner, or just someone trying to get more done in less time, this tool can fit into your life.

At its heart, DeepSeek uses advanced language models to understand your instructions and deliver results tailored to your needs. You type in a request—say, "Draft a thank-you note for a client" or "List ten marketing ideas for a coffee shop"—and it responds with polished, usable output. But it's not just a one-trick pony. DeepSeek can handle a wide range of tasks, from organizing your schedule to generating creative content to solving practical problems. The magic lies in its flexibility: you decide what you need, and it adapts to get it done.

What sets DeepSeek apart from other AI tools is its focus on user-friendliness. The interface is straightforward, the learning curve is gentle, and it's packed with features that make your life easier without overwhelming you. For example, you can save your favorite commands for quick access, tweak settings to match your style, or even build custom AI agents—more on those later. It's like having a Swiss Army knife for productivity, with tools for every job you can think of.

I first came across DeepSeek when I was buried under a mountain of emails and deadlines. I'd heard about AI but assumed it was for coders or big companies with deep pockets. Then a friend showed me how she used DeepSeek to automate her invoicing, and I was hooked. Within a day, I had it drafting responses to clients, and within a week, I was using it to plan my entire month. The best part? I didn't need to read a manual or watch endless tutorials. It just worked. That's what I want you to experience—a tool that feels intuitive and delivers results fast.

One thing to know upfront: DeepSeek isn't perfect. It's incredibly smart, but it's not a mind-reader. The quality of what you get depends on how clear your instructions are. Think of it like giving directions to a friend—if you're vague, they might take a wrong turn, but if you're specific, they'll get you exactly where you need to go. We'll talk more about how to give great instructions in later chapters, but for now, just know that DeepSeek is a partner, not a magic wand. With a little practice, you'll be amazed at what it can do.

Why AI Agents Are the Future of Work

You've probably noticed how fast technology is changing. From self-driving cars to voice assistants like Siri, AI is everywhere, and it's not slowing down. One of the most exciting developments is the rise of AI agents—customized programs you create to handle specific tasks automatically. Unlike a general-purpose tool like a calculator or a spreadsheet, an AI agent is tailored to your needs. Want it to reply to customer inquiries while you sleep? Done. Need it to track expenses and flag overspending? It can do that too. AI agents are like employees you design from scratch, except they work 24/7 and never ask for a raise.

Why are these agents such a big deal? For one, they save time—tons of it. Most of us spend hours every week on repetitive chores: sorting emails, updating calendars, pulling reports. An AI agent can take those off your plate, freeing you up to focus on what you're best at, whether that's designing, writing, or growing your business. I know a guy who runs a small bakery; he built an agent to handle online orders and cut his admin time from 20 hours a week to five. That's 15 extra hours he now spends experimenting with new recipes or hanging out with his kids.

Another reason AI agents are the future is their scalability. If you're a one-person operation, you can only do so much in a day. But an agent can handle hundreds or thousands of tasks at once, without breaking a sweat. Say you're a blogger who wants to post on social media daily. Instead of scheduling each post yourself, you can set up an agent to generate and share content automatically. If your audience grows, the agent keeps up, no extra effort required. It's like cloning yourself, but without the sci-fi ethical dilemmas.

AI agents also make work more creative. I used to think automation was just for boring, mechanical stuff, but I was wrong. Agents can brainstorm ideas, suggest improvements, even help you write a novel. Last year, I was stuck on a marketing campaign for a client. I built an agent to generate taglines based on my brand notes, and it came up with a winner I'd never have thought of on my own. By taking care of the grunt work, agents give you room to think bigger and bolder.

The best part? You don't need to be a tech expert to create these agents. DeepSeek makes it simple with templates and step-by-step options. You tell it what you want the agent to do, tweak a few settings, and let it run. It's like assembling a Lego set—snap the pieces together, and you've got something that works. As AI keeps evolving, agents will only get smarter, handling more complex jobs with less input from you. That's why getting started now puts you ahead of the curve. By learning to build and use agents today, you're setting yourself up for a future where work is less about drudgery and more about possibility.

How DeepSeek Can 10x Your Productivity

Let's talk about the big promise: 10x-ing your productivity. That might sound like hype, but stick with me—it's real, and I've seen it happen. Productivity isn't about working harder or cramming more into your day. It's about getting better results with less effort. DeepSeek helps you do that by speeding up tasks, cutting out wasted time, and helping you stay focused. Here's how it works in practice.

First, DeepSeek saves you time on routine tasks. Take writing, for example. Whether it's emails, reports, or social media posts, most of us spend hours typing away. With DeepSeek, you can generate a first draft in seconds. Just type something like, "Write a professional email inviting a client to a meeting," and you've got a polished version ready to tweak and send. I used to spend 30 minutes crafting replies to clients; now it's five minutes, tops. That adds up fast—hours saved every week.

Second, it helps you organize your life. DeepSeek can create schedules, prioritize tasks, or even remind you what needs doing. I'm a bit of a scatterbrain, so I used to rely on sticky notes and half-baked to-do lists. Now I ask DeepSeek to plan my week based on my goals, and it spits out a clear, actionable list. For instance, I might say, "List my top five priorities for the next three days, factoring in meetings and deadlines." The result is a roadmap that keeps me on track without the mental juggling act.

Third, DeepSeek boosts your decision-making. Ever get stuck choosing between options or figuring out the next step? You can ask it to analyze scenarios or suggest ideas. When I was launching a side hustle, I used DeepSeek to compare pricing strategies for my product. I fed it my costs and target market, and it gave me a breakdown of pros and cons for each option. It wasn't perfect, but it gave me clarity to move forward without second-guessing myself.

But here's the real game-changer: DeepSeek lets you batch tasks. Instead of doing one thing at a time, you can generate multiple outputs at once. Need ten blog post ideas, five email templates, and a week's worth of tweets? DeepSeek can handle it in one go. A friend of mine who runs an online store used this to create product descriptions for her entire catalog in an afternoon. What used to take her a month now takes a day. That's the kind of jump we're talking about—10x isn't just a number; it's a mindset shift.

Of course, it's not all smooth sailing. You'll need to experiment to find what works best for you. Early on, I tried using DeepSeek to write a presentation and got a wall of text that was way too formal. I learned to be specific— say, "Write a casual five-slide pitch for a small business audience." The more you use it, the better you get at asking for what you want. And don't worry about getting it perfect right away; even small wins, like cutting an hour off your workday, add up over time.

Setting Expectations for Beginners

If you're feeling a mix of excitement and nerves right now, you're not alone. Starting something new can be intimidating, especially when it's wrapped in buzzwords like "AI" and "automation." So let's set some realistic expectations to make this journey as smooth as possible. My aim is to help you avoid the pitfalls I hit when I was figuring out DeepSeek—and trust me, there were a few.

First off, expect a learning curve, but not a steep one. DeepSeek is designed to be beginner-friendly, with a clean layout and prompts that guide you along. You'll probably spend your first hour or two poking around, testing things out, and maybe chuckling at a few odd responses. That's normal. When I started, I asked DeepSeek to write a poem about my dog, and it gave me a 12-stanza epic that was hilariously over-the-top. Point is, you'll get the hang of it faster than you think, and every mistake is a chance to learn.

Second, don't expect DeepSeek to do everything for you. It's a tool, not a replacement for your brain. You'll still need to make decisions, refine outputs, and bring your own creativity to the table. Think of it like cooking with a fancy mixer—it makes the job easier, but you're still the chef. If you ask for a generic blog post, you'll get something usable but not spectacular. If you ask for a blog post tailored to your audience with a specific tone, you'll get something you can really work with. Your input shapes the outcome.

Third, plan to spend a little time upfront to save a lot later. Setting up DeepSeek—getting your account ready, exploring features, and maybe building your first agent—takes a bit of effort. I'd say give yourself a weekend to play around without pressure. Once you've got the basics down, the time you invest pays off in spades. I spent a Saturday messing with DeepSeek, and by Monday, I'd cut my email time in half. Small steps now lead to big wins down the road.

Finally, expect to be surprised. DeepSeek can do things you might not even think to ask for at first. I didn't realize I could use it to summarize long articles until a colleague mentioned it, and now it's one of my favorite tricks. As you read this book and try the prompts, you'll discover new ways to use the tool that fit your life. Keep an open mind, and don't be afraid to experiment. Some of my best results came from random "what if" moments, like when I asked DeepSeek to role-play as a customer to test my sales pitch.

One last thing: you don't need to master everything at once. This book is structured to guide you step by step, so you can focus on one piece at a time. Start with simple tasks, like drafting emails or making lists. As you get comfortable, move on to bigger stuff, like building agents or exploring business ideas. There's no rush—go at your own pace, and celebrate the progress along the way.

By now, you've got a clear picture of what DeepSeek is and why it's worth your time. It's a tool that can save you hours, spark new ideas, and even open doors to earning extra income. AI agents are changing how we work, and DeepSeek puts that power in your hands, no tech degree required. With the right approach, you can 10x your productivity, starting with small, practical steps. And as a beginner, you're not expected to know it all—just show up, try things out, and let the tool do the heavy lifting. In the next chapter, we'll get hands-on, walking you through how to set up DeepSeek and start using it for real. For now, take a moment to feel good about starting this journey. You're already one step closer to working smarter.

Chapter 2

Getting Started with DeepSeek

Alright, you've made it through the first chapter, and now it's time to roll up your sleeves and get hands-on with DeepSeek. This chapter is all about taking those first steps—setting up the tool, figuring out how it works, and getting comfortable with what it can do. I remember my own start with DeepSeek: I was eager but a little unsure, fumbling through the setup and wondering if I'd break something. Spoiler alert—I didn't, and you won't either. My goal here is to walk you through everything you need to begin, from creating your account to solving any hiccups that pop up. We'll cover how to get your DeepSeek environment ready, make sense of the interface and tools, highlight the features that matter most for beginners, and tackle common setup problems. By the end, you'll be ready to start using DeepSeek like it's second nature. Let's jump in and get you set up.

Setting Up Your DeepSeek Environment

Getting DeepSeek up and running is your first task, and it's easier than you might think. Whether you're on a laptop, desktop, or even a tablet, the process is straightforward. I'll guide you through it step by step, based on how I got started and what I've learned since. The aim is to have you ready to go in under an hour, with everything in place to start experimenting.

To begin, you'll need a device with internet access. DeepSeek is web-based, so there's no heavy software to download or install—just a browser like Chrome, Firefox, or Safari will do. Head to the official DeepSeek website (a quick search for "DeepSeek AI" should get you there). You'll see a homepage with a big "Sign Up" or "Get

Started" button—click that. If you can't find it, look in the top-right corner; websites love hiding things there. You'll be asked for an email address and a password. Pick something you'll remember, because you'll use it to log in every time. I went with my usual email and a password I scribbled on a sticky note (don't judge—it worked).

Once you submit your info, DeepSeek might send a confirmation email. Check your inbox—and your spam folder, just in case. Click the link in the email, and you're officially in. If you don't get an email after a few minutes, there's usually a "Resend" option on the login page. When I signed up, mine got buried in my promotions tab, so don't panic if it's not instant. After confirming, log in with your new credentials, and you'll land on the welcome screen. It might ask you to pick a plan—free or paid. The free version is fine for starting out; it gives you plenty of room to play around. I stuck with free for a month before upgrading, and it was more than enough to get the hang of things.

Next, you'll want to set up your workspace. DeepSeek greets you with a dashboard—a blank slate where you'll do most of your work. Take a minute to poke around. There's a text box where you type your requests, a menu on the side, and maybe a "Settings" or "Profile" area. Before you do anything else, check your internet connection. DeepSeek needs a steady signal to work smoothly, so if your Wi-Fi is spotty, plug into a wired connection or move closer to your router. I learned this the hard way when my first attempt stalled mid-sentence because my signal dropped.

Now, personalize it a bit. Look for a settings menu— usually a gear icon or your name in the corner. You can adjust things like language (English is default, but there are others), time zone, and notification preferences. I set mine to my local time so deadlines made sense, and I turned off email alerts because I didn't need my inbox pinging me every five minutes. If there's an option to save your work automatically, turn that on—it's a lifesaver if your browser crashes. DeepSeek might also offer a quick tutorial or tour. I skipped mine because I'm impatient, but if you're the cautious type, give it a watch. It's usually a two-minute rundown of the basics.

One pro tip: bookmark the DeepSeek login page in your browser. You'll be coming back a lot, and it's faster than searching every time. I also made a desktop shortcut by dragging the URL to my screen—little things like that save seconds that add up. If you're on a shared computer, log out when you're done to keep your account safe. With that, your environment is set. You've got a functional DeepSeek setup, ready for action. It's not fancy, but it's yours, and that's what counts.

Understanding the Interface and Tools

Now that you're logged in, let's make sense of what you're looking at. The DeepSeek interface might feel unfamiliar at first, but it's built to be simple once you know the layout. Think of it like a new phone—you'll fumble for a day, then wonder how you ever lived without it. I'll break it down piece by piece, based on what I saw when I started and how I use it now. The goal is to get you comfortable navigating and using the tools without second-guessing yourself.

The dashboard is your home base. At the center, there's a big text box—sometimes labeled "Ask" or "Prompt"—where you type what you want DeepSeek to do. It's the heart of the whole operation. Try typing something basic, like "List five dinner ideas." Hit enter, and a response pops up below or in a new window. When I first tried it, I asked for "Ten ways to organize my desk," and it gave me a solid list in seconds. That's your main interaction point—type, hit enter, get results.

On the left or right, you'll see a sidebar. This is your toolbox. It might have options like "History," "Saved," or "Agents." "History" shows past requests, which is handy if you forget what you asked earlier. I use it to revisit prompts that worked well—like the time I had DeepSeek draft a pitch and wanted to reuse it. "Saved" is for storing responses you like; click a star or button next to an output to keep it there. The "Agents" section is where you'll build custom helpers later—we'll get to that in Chapter 4. For now, just note where it is.

At the top, there's usually a bar with your profile name, a logout button, and maybe a help icon. Click your name to tweak settings or check your account status (like how many free uses you have left). The help icon might link to FAQs or a support chat—useful if you're stuck. I ignored it at first, but when I couldn't figure out why my text kept disappearing, the FAQ saved me (turns out I was hitting "clear" by accident). If there's a search bar, it's for finding old prompts or features—type "email" to see past email drafts, for example.

The tools themselves are what you access through that text box. DeepSeek can write, list, summarize, calculate, and more, depending on what you ask. It's not a separate app for each task—it's all in how you phrase your request. For instance, "Summarize this article" followed by a pasted link gets you a quick recap. "Plan a week of workouts" gets you a schedule. I once asked, "Write a funny tweet about Mondays," and got a gem that made my coworkers laugh. The trick is experimenting to see what sticks.

One thing to watch: the interface might shift slightly depending on updates. When I started, the sidebar was on the left; a month later, it moved right. Don't let that throw you—just look for the labels. If something looks off, refresh the page. DeepSeek runs online, so it's tied to their servers, and a quick reload usually fixes quirks. Spend 10 minutes clicking around, typing random requests, and you'll feel at home. It's less about memorizing and more about getting a feel for it.

Key Features for Beginners

DeepSeek is packed with features, but as a beginner, you don't need to know them all yet. I'll focus on the ones that'll give you the most bang for your buck right away. These are the tools I leaned on when I was new, and they're still my go-tos. They're simple, practical, and perfect for building confidence as you learn.

First up: text generation. This is DeepSeek's bread and butter. You can use it to write anything—emails, notes, blog posts, even grocery lists. Just tell it what you want and how you want it. For example, "Write a short email thanking a friend for a gift" gets you a ready-to-send message. I used this to draft a proposal for a client in 10 minutes instead of an hour. Play with tone too—add "casual" or "formal" to match your style. It's not flawless, but it's a huge time-saver.

Next, list-making. DeepSeek loves lists. Ask it to brainstorm ideas, outline steps, or prioritize tasks. I started with "List ten ways to save time at work," and it gave me solid suggestions I still use, like batching emails. You can get specific—say, "List five healthy snacks under 200 calories"—and it'll tailor the output. It's like having a personal idea machine that never runs dry.

Another gem: summarization. If you've got a long article, report, or email thread, paste it in and ask DeepSeek to shorten it. "Summarize this in three sentences" works wonders. I used this when a coworker sent me a 1,000-word project update—I got the gist in 30 seconds. It's not perfect for super technical stuff, but for everyday reading, it's a game-changer.

Then there's scheduling. DeepSeek can plan your day, week, or month based on what you tell it. Try "Create a Monday schedule with work from 9-5 and a gym break at 3." It'll spit out a timeline you can tweak. I did this for a hectic week of deadlines and family stuff, and it kept me sane. It won't sync with your calendar (yet), but it's a solid starting point.

Finally, basic problem-solving. DeepSeek can help with quick fixes or decisions. Ask, "How do I fix a slow computer?" or "Should I buy this phone based on these specs?" and it'll give you practical advice. I once asked it to compare two job offers by salary and hours—it wasn't definitive, but it helped me think it through. Keep questions simple at first; complex stuff comes later.

These features are your foundation. They're easy to use, don't need fancy setup, and show off what DeepSeek can do without overwhelming you. Start with one—say, text generation—and mess around until you're happy. Then try another. You'll build momentum fast.

Troubleshooting Common Setup Issues

Even with a tool as user-friendly as DeepSeek, things can go sideways. Don't worry—I've hit most of these snags myself, and they're all fixable. This section is your safety net for when the setup doesn't go as planned. I'll cover the problems beginners often face, how to spot them, and what to do, based on my own stumbles and fixes.

First issue: login trouble. If you can't sign in, double-check your email and password. Typos are sneaky—I once typed ".con" instead of ".com" and spent 10 minutes cursing before I noticed. If it's correct but still fails, use the "Forgot Password" link. You'll get a reset email—check spam if it's not in your inbox. When I had this, it took two tries because my Wi-Fi was lagging, so test your connection too.

Second: blank screen or loading errors. After logging in, you might see nothing but a spinning wheel or a white page. This usually means a server hiccup or browser glitch. Refresh the page first—hit F5 or the reload button. If that flops, clear your browser cache. On Chrome, go to Settings, Privacy, "Clear Browsing Data," and pick "Cached Images and Files." I had to do this once when

DeepSeek froze mid-response; it took two minutes and worked like a charm. If it's still dead, try a different browser.

Third: prompts not working. You type a request, hit enter, and… nothing. Or maybe you get an error like "Invalid Input." Check your internet—DeepSeek needs it to process. If that's fine, simplify your request. I asked, "Write a 50-page novel about pirates," and got an error because it was too big. "Write a pirate story in 100 words" worked fine. Start small and build up. If it's still broken, log out and back in—sometimes the session just needs a reset.

Fourth: missing features. You might look for "Saved" or "Agents" and not see them. This could mean you're on the free plan, which limits some tools. Check your account status under your profile—look for "Plan" or "Subscription." The free tier is great, but paid unlocks more. When I couldn't find the agent builder, I realized I needed to upgrade. If you're paid and still missing stuff, contact support via the help link. They're slow sometimes, but they'll sort it.

Last: slow performance. If DeepSeek lags or takes forever to respond, it's usually your device or connection. Close other tabs—ten open YouTube videos will tank anything. I had this when I was streaming music and working; shutting Spotify fixed it. If your computer's old, lower the browser's memory use (Google "reduce browser memory" for your brand). Worst case, it's DeepSeek's servers— wait a few minutes and retry.

For anything else, the help section or a quick online search (try "DeepSeek [your issue]") usually has answers. I once couldn't save a prompt and found a forum post saying to click the star twice—random, but it worked. Keep calm, try these fixes, and you'll be back on track. Setup hiccups are normal; they don't mean you're doing it wrong.

You're now officially started with DeepSeek. Your environment's ready, you know the interface and tools, you've got beginner-friendly features to play with, and you can handle any setup bumps. It's like moving into a new place—takes a bit to settle in, but soon it feels like home. Next chapter, we'll build on this, showing you how to use DeepSeek to slash your workload and boost your day-to-day output. For now, pat yourself on the back—you've got the basics down, and that's a big win.

Chapter 3

Mastering Productivity with DeepSeek

You've got DeepSeek set up and you're familiar with how it works—now it's time to put it to use and supercharge your productivity. This chapter is where the rubber meets the road. I remember when I first started playing with DeepSeek beyond the basics; I was amazed at how much time I could save and how much smoother my days felt. That's what I want for you here. We're going to explore practical ways to make your work faster, easier, and less stressful.

I'll share my top 10 productivity hacks that turned me into a DeepSeek fan, show you how to automate those annoying repetitive tasks, explain how to manage your time better with AI help, and give you over 200 prompts you can use every day. This isn't about theory—it's about real, hands-on stuff you can try right now. Let's get started and make your days work for you.

Top 10 Productivity Hacks Using DeepSeek

Productivity isn't about doing more; it's about doing what matters with less effort. DeepSeek has become my secret weapon for that, and these 10 hacks are the best tricks I've found. They're simple, tested by me and others, and perfect for anyone just getting comfortable with the tool. Let's walk through them.

1. Batch Email Drafts: Writing emails one by one is a time sink. Instead, I use DeepSeek to draft a bunch at once. Try typing, "Write five short emails: one thanking a client, one rescheduling a meeting, one following up on a payment, one asking for

feedback, and one confirming a deadline." You'll get five solid drafts in under a minute. I tweak them to fit the person and hit send. What used to take an hour now takes 15 minutes.

2. Brainstorm in Seconds: Stuck on ideas? DeepSeek can spit out lists fast. I'll say, "Give me ten blog post topics for a fitness site," and boom—ten ideas I can pick from or mix up. It's like having a creative buddy who never gets tired. I used this for a friend's podcast, and we had a month's worth of episodes planned in 10 minutes.

3. Turn Notes into Plans: I'm terrible at organizing raw thoughts. If I've got a messy list—like "call Tom, finish report, groceries, gym"—I ask DeepSeek, "Turn this into a prioritized to-do list for today: [paste notes]." It sorts them by urgency and even suggests times. Saved me from forgetting a client call last week.

4. Quick Summaries: Reading long stuff eats time. I paste articles or emails into DeepSeek and say, "Summarize this in three bullet points." I did this

with a 20-page industry report and got the key points in 30 seconds. It's not deep analysis, but it keeps me in the loop without bogging me down.

5. Script Routine Calls: Phone calls can drag on. Before I call someone, I ask DeepSeek, "Write a 60-second script for a call to confirm a delivery date." It gives me a clear outline—intro, question, close—so I stay on track. I used this for a supplier chat and wrapped up in two minutes instead of ten.

6. Pre-Write Social Posts: Posting daily is a chore. I tell DeepSeek, "Create seven casual tweets about coffee," and get a week's worth ready to schedule. I tweak them to sound like me, but the heavy lifting's done. A café owner I know does this for Instagram and says it's cut her prep time in half.

7. Polish Rough Drafts: My writing's messy at first. I'll jot down a rough email or post, then ask DeepSeek, "Make this clearer and more professional: [paste text]." It smooths out the edges without changing my voice. I used this for a pitch to a client, and they signed on the next day.

8. Plan Meals Fast: Cooking takes planning. I say, "List five dinners with chicken, under 30 minutes to make," and DeepSeek hands me recipes with steps. I started doing this weekly, and it's killed my "what's for dinner" stress. Bonus: my grocery list is half-done too.

9. Break Down Big Tasks: Big projects overwhelm me. I'll type, "Break this into five steps: finish a 10-page presentation by Friday." DeepSeek gives me a plan—research, outline, draft, design, review—with deadlines. I used this for a work deck and hit my goal without panicking.

10. Quick Answers: Googling takes forever sometimes. I ask DeepSeek, "How do I fix a printer jam?" or "What's the best free app for notes?" and get a straight answer. It's not always perfect, but it's faster than sifting through ads. Saved me 20 minutes when my Wi-Fi died last month.

These hacks are my go-tos because they're quick wins. Pick one, try it today, and see the difference. They're not complicated—just smart ways to use what DeepSeek offers.

Automating Repetitive Tasks

Repetitive tasks are the silent killers of productivity—boring, endless, and always creeping back. DeepSeek can take them off your hands with automation, and I'll show you how. I used to spend hours on stuff like data entry or formatting, but now I let DeepSeek handle it. Here's how to make that happen for you.

Start with identifying what you repeat. For me, it was typing the same email responses—like "Thanks for your order, here's the next step." I'd send 10 a day, eating up 30 minutes. Now, I use DeepSeek to pre-write them. Type, "Create a reusable template for an order confirmation email," and save the result. Next time, I just paste it, tweak the name, and send. It's down to two minutes total.

Another big one: data sorting. If you track anything—expenses, client info, sales—DeepSeek can organize it. I used to manually log receipts in a spreadsheet. Now, I paste a list like "coffee $5, gas $30, lunch $12" and say, "Sort this into a table with columns for item and cost." It builds the table in seconds, and I copy it to Excel. A friend who freelances does this with client hours—saves her an hour a week.

Formatting is a pain too. Say you write reports or posts that need consistent headers, bullets, spacing. I'd spend 15 minutes per report fixing that. Now, I dump my rough text into DeepSeek and say, "Format this as a professional report with headings and bullets." It's done in a flash, and I just adjust as needed. A coworker used this for meeting notes and cut her cleanup time from 20 minutes to five.

You can also automate reminders. I forget follow-ups constantly. I ask DeepSeek, "List my tasks—email Jen, call Mike, finish doc—and turn them into a reminder list with times for tomorrow." It gives me a schedule I paste into my phone. It's not a full calendar sync, but it beats forgetting. I did this for a project and stayed on top of every deadline.

The key to automation is specificity. Tell DeepSeek exactly what to do—don't just say "help me with emails." I learned this when I asked for "a template" and got something vague. "Write a 50-word template for a payment reminder email" got me what I needed. Test it, save what works, and reuse it. Soon, you'll have a library of shortcuts for all your repeat offenders.

Time Management with AI Assistance

Time slips away too easily, but DeepSeek can help you grab it back. I used to think I was "busy" all day, only to realize half my hours went to distractions or poor planning. With DeepSeek, I've gotten better at managing my time, and you can too. Here's how it's worked for me and how to make it work for you.

First, use DeepSeek to plan your day. I start mornings by typing, "Plan my day: work 9-5, lunch at noon, gym at 3, finish report by 4." It spits out a schedule—9-12 work, 12-1 lunch, 1-3 work, 3-4 gym, 4-5 report. I tweak it if needed, but it's a solid start. A buddy who's a student does this for classes and study blocks—keeps him from cramming.

Second, prioritize tasks. I'll list what's on my plate—"email client, design flyer, call supplier, prep meeting"—and say, "Rank these by urgency, due today." DeepSeek orders them based on what I tell it, like "email client first, due at 11." I used this during a crunch week and hit every deadline without stressing.

Third, track your time. I'm bad at guessing how long things take. Now, I ask DeepSeek, "Estimate time for these: write a 500-word post, call a friend, shop online." It guesses—say, 30 minutes, 10 minutes, 20 minutes—and I use that to pace myself. It's not exact, but it's close enough. I did this for a side gig and stopped overbooking myself.

Fourth, block distractions. DeepSeek can't shut off your phone, but it can help you focus. I say, "Write a 25-minute work plan with no breaks," and it gives me a mini-schedule—10 minutes email, 10 minutes drafting, 5 minutes review. I follow it with a timer, and it's like a mini Pomodoro. A colleague uses this for writing and says it's doubled her output.

The trick is consistency. Use DeepSeek daily for planning, and you'll see patterns—like how mornings are your best work hours. I started small, just scheduling afternoons, and now I plan full weeks. It's not about rigid rules; it's about knowing where your time goes and making it count.

200+ Productivity Prompts for Everyday Use

Prompts are how you tell DeepSeek what to do, and I've got over 200 here to save you time every day. These are ones I've used, refined, and shared with friends—they work. I'll list them by category with examples, so you can grab what fits your life. Copy them, tweak them, make them yours.

Emails Prompts

- "Write a 50-word email thanking a client for their business."
- "Draft a polite email rescheduling a meeting to next Tuesday at 10 AM."
- "Create a follow-up email for an unpaid invoice, due last week."
- "Write a casual email asking a friend for a favor."
- "Compose a professional email confirming a project deadline of Friday."

- "Send a quick email apologizing for a delay in shipping an order."
- "Write a friendly email inviting a coworker to lunch next week."
- "Draft a 50-word email requesting feedback on a recent presentation."
- "Create a short email declining a meeting invite due to a conflict."
- "Compose an email asking a supplier for a delivery update."
- "Write a professional email introducing yourself to a new client."
- "Draft a casual email checking in on a friend's weekend plans."
- "Create a polite email asking a teammate to review a document."
- "Write a 50-word email thanking a vendor for quick service."
- "Compose an email confirming a phone call appointment for tomorrow."

- "Send a brief email requesting a deadline extension from a boss."
- "Draft a friendly email congratulating a colleague on a promotion."
- "Write a short email asking a client to confirm a payment method."
- "Create a professional email scheduling a site visit for next Monday."
- "Compose a casual email thanking a neighbor for help with a task."

Task Lists Prompts

- "Turn this into a to-do list: call mom, shop, finish email, gym."
- "List five priorities for today based on: report due, meeting at 2, lunch."
- "Create a weekend task list with: clean, read, cook, relax."
- "Sort these by urgency: email boss, pay bill, plan trip."

- "Make a daily checklist for: work 9-5, exercise, dinner."
- "Turn this into a prioritized list: finish homework, call friend, laundry, study."
- "List four tasks for this afternoon: reply to emails, prep meeting, walk dog, shop."
- "Create a Monday to-do list with: work 8-4, gym, cook dinner, read."
- "Sort these by deadline: submit form by noon, call by 3, email tonight."
- "Make a checklist for a busy day: meetings 10-12, lunch, report, errands."
- "Turn this into a simple list: water plants, pay rent, write note, nap."
- "List five morning tasks based on: breakfast, emails, plan day, exercise."
- "Create a task list for a trip prep: pack, book hotel, check car, shop."
- "Sort these by importance: fix printer, call client, update calendar."

- "Make a daily plan for: work 9-3, lunch, gym, family time."
- "Turn this into a to-do list: bake cookies, call sister, clean desk, relax."
- "List three priorities for tonight: finish project, email team, rest."
- "Create a weekend checklist with: grocery shop, hike, call parents, chores."
- "Sort these by time needed: write letter, buy gift, schedule appointment."
- "Make a task list for a work-from-home day: emails, calls, lunch, report."

Brainstorming Prompts

- "Give me ten blog ideas for a travel site."
- "List five ways to promote a small bakery."
- "Suggest ten gifts for a 30-year-old's birthday."
- "Generate five slogans for a pet store."
- "List ten topics for a cooking YouTube channel."
- "Provide ten ideas for a fitness Instagram account."

- "Suggest five ways to advertise a local coffee shop."
- "List ten activities for a family weekend at home."
- "Generate five taglines for a handmade jewelry business."
- "Give me ten podcast episode ideas about personal finance."
- "Suggest ten themes for a photography blog."
- "List five marketing ideas for a freelance writing service."
- "Provide ten gift ideas for a teacher's appreciation day."
- "Generate five catchphrases for a fitness gym."
- "List ten video ideas for a gardening YouTube channel."
- "Suggest five ways to boost sales at a bookstore."
- "Give me ten blog post ideas for a parenting website."
- "List ten creative date night ideas for couples."
- "Generate five mottos for a sustainable clothing brand."

- "Provide ten topics for a DIY home improvement podcast."
- "Suggest five promotion ideas for a new restaurant opening."
- "List ten gift suggestions for a tech enthusiast."
- "Generate five slogans for a car repair shop."
- "Give me ten ideas for a mental health awareness campaign."
- "List ten topics for a beginner's art tutorial series."
- "Suggest five ways to grow a dog grooming business."
- "Provide ten blog ideas for a fashion tips site."
- "Generate five taglines for a travel agency."
- "List ten activities for a team-building event."
- "Suggest five ideas to increase followers on a foodie Instagram."

Writing Prompts
- "Write a 100-word bio for a graphic designer."
- "Draft a 200-word post about morning routines."

- "Create a 50-word ad for a yoga class."
- "Polish this rough note into a clear paragraph: [paste text]."
- "Write a funny 280-character tweet about rain."
- "Compose a 150-word about page for a small bakery website."
- "Write a 50-word product description for a handmade candle."
- "Draft a 100-word review of a recent movie."
- "Create a 280-character motivational quote for a Monday."
- "Rewrite this sentence to sound friendlier: [paste text]."
- "Write a 200-word blog post about the benefits of walking."
- "Compose a 50-word flyer for a local book club."
- "Draft a 100-word thank-you note for a wedding gift."
- "Create a funny 50-word caption for a dog photo."
- "Write a 150-word FAQ section for a coffee shop."

- "Polish this rough email into a professional version: [paste text]."
- "Compose a 200-word post about organizing a home office."
- "Write a 50-word ad for a dog walking service."
- "Draft a 100-word bio for a freelance photographer."
- "Create a 280-character tweet about a sunny day."
- "Write a 150-word customer testimonial for a gym."
- "Rewrite this paragraph to be shorter and clearer: [paste text]."
- "Compose a 200-word article about saving money on groceries."
- "Write a 50-word invite for a community cleanup event."
- "Draft a 100-word LinkedIn post about a work milestone."
- "Create a funny 50-word story about a lost sock."
- "Write a 150-word description for a travel tour package."

- "Polish this rough ad into a catchy version: [paste text]."
- "Compose a 200-word post about staying productive at home."
- "Write a 50-word tagline and intro for a pet adoption event."

Planning Prompts

- "Plan my day: work 8-4, lunch at 12, call at 2."
- "Create a week schedule: work M-F, gym T/Th, family Sunday."
- "Break this into steps: launch a blog by month-end."
- "Estimate time for: write email, shop, cook dinner."
- "Schedule a Saturday: errands 10-12, relax 1-3, movie 7."
- "Plan my morning: breakfast 7, emails 8, meeting 9-10."
- "Create a three-day schedule: work M-W, gym M, errands W."

- "Break this into steps: finish a work project by Friday."
- "Estimate time for: call client, draft post, walk dog."
- "Schedule a Sunday: church 9-11, lunch 12, nap 2-3."
- "Plan my week: work 9-5 M-F, dinner date Th, hike Sat."
- "Create a daily routine: wake 6, work 8-4, gym 5."
- "Break this into steps: plan a birthday party by next week."
- "Estimate time for: shop groceries, cook meal, clean kitchen."
- "Schedule a Friday: work 9-3, coffee with friend 4, movie 8."
- "Plan my afternoon: emails 1-2, report 2-4, break 4-5."
- "Create a weekend plan: clean Sat 10-12, relax Sun all day."
- "Break this into steps: start a podcast by next month."
- "Estimate time for: write note, pay bills, call mom."

- "Schedule a Tuesday: work 8-5, gym 6, dinner with family 7."
- "Plan my day: work from home 9-5, lunch 1, walk 3."
- "Create a week schedule: work M-Th, gym W/F, rest Sat-Sun."
- "Break this into steps: organize a garage sale by Saturday."
- "Estimate time for: draft email, shop online, prep lunch."
- "Schedule a Monday: meetings 10-12, lunch 1, emails 2-4."
- "Plan my evening: cook 6-7, read 7-8, TV 8-10."
- "Create a three-day plan: work Th-Sat, gym Fri, family Sat."
- "Break this into steps: complete a school assignment by Wed."
- "Estimate time for: call friend, write post, tidy room."
- "Schedule a weekend: shop Sat 11-1, hike Sun 2-4, relax."

Summaries Prompts

- "Summarize this in two sentences: [paste article]."
- "Give me three bullet points for this email: [paste text]."
- "Shorten this report to 50 words: [paste report]."
- "List key points from this meeting note: [paste note]."
- "Condense this news story into one paragraph: [paste story]."
- "Reduce this blog post to three main ideas: [paste post]."
- "Summarize this book chapter in 75 words: [paste chapter]."
- "Give me four highlights from this speech: [paste speech]."
- "Shorten this email thread to two key points: [paste thread]."
- "List three takeaways from this article: [paste article]."
- "Condense this project update into 50 words: [paste update]."

- "Summarize this podcast episode in one paragraph: [paste transcript]."
- "Give me two bullet points for this memo: [paste memo]."
- "Shorten this review to 25 words: [paste review]."
- "List key details from this customer feedback: [paste feedback]."
- "Reduce this news report to three sentences: [paste report]."
- "Summarize this instruction manual in 100 words: [paste manual]."
- "Give me three main points from this presentation: [paste slides]."
- "Condense this interview into two paragraphs: [paste interview]."
- "Shorten this policy document to four highlights: [paste document]."

Daily Life Prompts
- "List five quick dinners with beef."

- "Write a grocery list for a week of meals."
- "Plan a 20-minute workout with no equipment."
- "Suggest five ways to relax after work."
- "Create a packing list for a weekend trip."
- "List five breakfast ideas with eggs."
- "Write a shopping list for a family barbecue."
- "Plan a 15-minute stretching routine for mornings."
- "Suggest five activities for a rainy day indoors."
- "Create a checklist for cleaning the kitchen."
- "List five easy lunches with chicken."
- "Write a grocery list for a vegetarian week."
- "Plan a 30-minute bodyweight workout for home."
- "Suggest five ways to unwind before bed."
- "Create a packing list for a beach day."
- "List five snacks under 100 calories."
- "Write a shopping list for a holiday dinner."
- "Plan a 10-minute warm-up for running."
- "Suggest five ideas for a fun family night."
- "Create a checklist for morning chores."
- "List five dinners using pantry staples."
- "Write a grocery list for a camping trip."

- "Plan a 25-minute yoga session for beginners."
- "Suggest five ways to stay cool in summer."
- "Create a packing list for a business trip."
- "List five quick breakfasts for busy mornings."
- "Write a shopping list for a week of healthy snacks."
- "Plan a 20-minute cardio workout with no gear."
- "Suggest five activities for a solo weekend."
- "Create a checklist for evening wind-down."
- "List five meals with fish for dinner."
- "Write a grocery list for a potluck party."
- "Plan a 15-minute core workout at home."
- "Suggest five ways to boost energy in the afternoon."
- "Create a packing list for a hiking day."
- "List five desserts with five ingredients or less."
- "Write a shopping list for a kid's birthday party."
- "Plan a 30-minute walk-and-stretch routine."
- "Suggest five ideas for a cozy night in."
- "Create a checklist for weekly meal prep."
- "List five lunches to pack for work."

- "Write a grocery list for a low-budget week."
- "Plan a 10-minute cool-down after exercise."
- "Suggest five ways to organize a small closet."
- "Create a packing list for a cold-weather trip."
- "List five breakfast smoothies with fruit."
- "Write a shopping list for a soup-and-salad week."
- "Plan a 20-minute workout for upper body strength."
- "Suggest five ways to make mornings less rushed."
- "Create a checklist for a car maintenance day."

You're now armed to master productivity with DeepSeek. These hacks, automation tricks, time management tips, and prompts are your toolkit to get more done with less hassle. I've seen it transform my days—less chaos, more control—and I know it can do the same for you. Next chapter, we'll take it up a notch and build your first AI agent. For now, try a hack or prompt today and enjoy the win.

Chapter 4

Building Your First AI Agent

You've made it this far—congratulations! By now, you're comfortable with DeepSeek, using it to save time and get organized. But here's where things get really exciting: building your first AI agent. When I first heard about agents, I pictured something out of a sci-fi movie—complicated and way beyond my skills. Then I tried it with DeepSeek, and I couldn't believe how simple it was to create something that worked for me around the clock. This chapter is your guide to that process.

We'll start by explaining what AI agents are and how they function, then walk you through creating one step by step. After that, I'll show you how to tweak your agent for specific jobs, and wrap up with over 150 prompts to help you build agents that get stuff done. This is hands-on, practical stuff—based on my own experience and what I've seen work for others. Let's get into it and make your first agent a reality.

What Are AI Agents and How Do They Work?

AI agents sound fancy, but they're just helpers you design to handle tasks automatically. Think of them as little workers you train to do specific jobs—like answering emails, tracking data, or posting updates—without you lifting a finger after setup. I used to think automation was only for tech wizards, but DeepSeek makes it so anyone can build an agent. Let's break down what they are and how they tick, so you're clear on what's possible.

An AI agent is a custom program you create within DeepSeek. Unlike the one-off requests you've been typing—like "write an email"—an agent sticks around, ready to run its task whenever you need it. Say you want something to check your inbox every morning and draft replies to common questions. You set up an agent for that, give it instructions, and it does the job on its own. I built one to sort my freelance invoices, and now I don't waste an hour every week chasing payments.

How do they work? DeepSeek uses its smarts—those same language skills you've been using—to power agents. You tell it what to do with a prompt, like "Find emails with 'urgent' and write a polite reply." The agent takes that instruction, applies it to whatever you point it at (like your email account, if connected), and delivers results. It's not magic—it's just following your rules, but it feels like having an extra pair of hands. My first agent was a simple one that listed my daily tasks from a messy note; it wasn't perfect, but it saved me 20 minutes of sorting.

Agents can be basic or fancy, depending on what you ask. A basic one might just organize a list, while a fancier one could monitor a website and alert you to changes—if

DeepSeek supports that hookup. Most beginner agents don't need outside connections; they work with what you type or upload. I started with one that turned my scribbled ideas into neat project steps, all inside DeepSeek's dashboard. No coding, no tech degree—just clear directions.

The beauty of agents is they run on their own once you set them up. You don't have to keep typing the same prompt daily; the agent remembers and repeats. For example, I've got one that drafts social media posts every Monday from a list of topics I gave it. I check the output, tweak if needed, and post. It's like training a dog—teach it once, and it fetches whenever you say "go." DeepSeek handles the heavy lifting; you just decide what needs lifting.

One catch: agents aren't flawless. They depend on your instructions being clear. I once made an agent to summarize articles but forgot to say "keep it short"—I got 500-word essays instead of paragraphs. Lesson learned— be specific. They also can't do everything; if DeepSeek doesn't connect to your apps yet, your agent's limited to what you feed it manually. Still, even basic agents can save you hours, and that's what we're aiming for here.

Step-by-Step Guide to Creating an Agent in DeepSeek

Ready to build your first agent? I'll walk you through it, step by step, based on how I made mine and what I've figured out since. This isn't guesswork—it's what worked for me, and it'll work for you too. We'll create a simple agent to start, something useful but not overwhelming. Let's do this together.

- **Step 1: Log In and Find the Agent Section** - Open DeepSeek in your browser and sign in. Look at the sidebar—you'll see an option like "Agents" or "Create Agent." It might be under a menu if the layout's changed, so hunt around. When I started, it was on the left; now it's sometimes a tab at the top. Click it, and you'll land on a page with a "New Agent" button or similar. Hit that to begin.

- **Step 2: Name Your Agent** - You'll get a box to name it. Pick something clear—like "Task Lister" if it's organizing tasks, or "Email Responder" if it's drafting replies. I called my first one "Daily Planner" because it sorted my day. Keep it short; you'll recognize it later when you've got a few agents running. Type the name and save or move to the next step—there's usually a "Next" button.

- **Step 3: Define the Task** - Here's where you tell it what to do. You'll see a text field labeled something like "Instructions" or "Prompt." This is the heart of your agent. For our example, let's make a "Task Lister" that turns messy notes into a to-do list. Type: "Take my daily notes and make a numbered to-do list, sorted by what I need to do first." Keep it simple but specific—I messed up my first try by saying "organize my stuff," and it just rewrote my notes in a random order. Hit "Save" or "Continue."

- **Step 4: Add Input (If Needed)** - Some agents need input to work—like a note to sort or a file to process. DeepSeek might ask, "What's the input?" For our Task Lister, you'd paste a sample note, like "call Jen, shop, finish report, lunch." I did this so my agent knew what to expect. If there's an "Add Input" or "Test Data" option, use it. If not, you'll feed it later when you run the agent. Save your progress.

- **Step 5: Test It Out** - Look for a "Test" or "Run" button. Click it, and DeepSeek will show what your agent does with the input. For my Daily Planner, I got a list: "1. Finish report, 2. Call Jen, 3. Lunch, 4. Shop." It guessed priority based on common sense—not perfect, but close. If yours flops—like mine did when it listed "lunch" first—go back to Step 3 and tweak the prompt. Maybe add "put work tasks before meals." Test again until it's right.

- **Step 6: Save and Activate** - Once it works, hit "Save Agent" or "Finish." You might see an "Activate" toggle—turn it on so the agent's ready to use. DeepSeek stores it in your agent list. I forgot to save once and had to redo it, so don't skip this. If there's a "Schedule" option, you can set it to run daily or weekly—mine runs every morning now, but for now, leave it manual.

- **Step 7: Run It Anytime** - Back on the agent page, find your Task Lister. Click it, paste new notes—like "email boss, gym, pay bill"—and hit "Run." You'll get a fresh list. I use mine daily; it's not fancy, but it saves me 10 minutes of head-scratching. If it's off, adjust the prompt and test again. You've got an agent now—congrats!

That's it—seven steps, and you're done. It took me 15 minutes the first time, including a few do-overs. Start with this Task Lister, then play with others as you get the hang of it. DeepSeek makes it forgiving—you can edit anytime if it's not perfect.

Customizing Your Agent for Specific Tasks

Your first agent is running, but the real fun is making it fit your exact needs. Customization is where agents shine—you turn a basic helper into something that feels made just for you. I'll show you how I tweaked mine and give you ideas to tailor yours, based on real examples that worked for me and folks I know.

Start by refining the prompt. My Task Lister was okay, but it kept putting "relax" before "work," which wasn't helpful. I changed it to: "Make a numbered to-do list from my notes, sorting work tasks first, then personal, and meals last." Tested it with "call client, nap, lunch, write post," and got "1. Call client, 2. Write post, 3. Nap, 4. Lunch." Spot on. Go to your agent, edit the instructions, and test with your own notes—add rules like "urgent tasks first" if that's your style.

Next, adjust the output. DeepSeek might let you pick formats—like bullets, numbers, or paragraphs. My Daily

Planner defaulted to numbers, but I tried "Format as bullet points instead." Now it's "- Call client, - Write post," etc.—easier to read on my phone. Check your agent settings for a "Style" or "Output" option. If not, add it to the prompt: "List tasks as bullets." I helped a friend set hers to "short sentences" for a report generator—small tweak, big difference.

You can also limit or expand scope. My Task Lister handled daily stuff fine, but I wanted one for weekly projects. I edited it to: "Turn my weekly goals into a task list, split by day, work first." Input became "finish deck, call team, shop, rest," and output was "Mon: Finish deck, Tue: Call team, Wed: Shop, Thu: Rest." If yours is too broad, narrow it—like "only email tasks"—or widen it for more jobs. Test with your own goals.

Add conditions if DeepSeek allows. Some setups let you say, "Run only if I type 'urgent'" or "Use this list on Mondays." Mine's basic, so I manually paste notes, but check your agent page for "Triggers" or "Rules." A buddy made his "Sales Tracker" scan a spreadsheet only when updated—fancy, but optional for now. Start simple; you can grow into that.

Finally, name it something personal. "Task Lister" is fine, but "My Day Fixer" feels mine. I renamed mine "Work First Planner" to match its job. Edit the name in settings—it's a small touch that makes it yours. Customization is trial and error; tweak, test, tweak again. My friend's "Email Buddy" went through three versions before it nailed client replies—patience pays off.

150+ Prompts to Build Effective AI Agents

Prompts are the backbone of your agents, and I've got over 150 here to get you started. These are ones I've used or seen work, refined to be clear and effective. They're grouped by type—task organizers, content creators, trackers, responders—so you can pick what fits. Each one's a ready-to-go instruction; just plug it into your agent setup and adjust as needed. Let's roll.

Task Organizers Prompts

- "Turn my daily notes into a numbered to-do list, work first, personal last."
- "Sort my tasks by urgency from this: call boss, shop, finish report."
- "Make a weekly plan from my goals: write post, gym, family time."
- "List my tasks as bullets, split into morning and afternoon: [paste notes]."
- "Create a daily checklist from: emails, meeting, lunch, gym."
- "Organize my weekend tasks: clean, read, cook, sorted by time needed."
- "Turn my messy list into steps: launch site, email team, shop."
- "Sort my to-dos by deadline: pay bill tomorrow, call Fri, email today."

- "Make a task list for today: work 9-5, break 12, call 3."
- "Break my project into daily tasks: finish book by month-end."
- "List my chores as a checklist: laundry, dishes, vacuum."
- "Sort my errands by location: bank, store, post office."
- "Create a morning routine from: breakfast, emails, walk."
- "Turn my notes into a priority list: [paste notes], urgent first."
- "Plan my week from: work M-F, gym T/Th, rest Sun."
- "List my tasks in order: call client, write memo, lunch."
- "Make a to-do list for a trip: pack, book, check car."
- "Sort my goals by effort: small tasks first, big last."
- "Create a daily plan: work 8-4, gym 5, dinner 6."
- "Turn my ideas into steps: start blog, pick name, write post."

- "List my evening tasks: cook, read, TV, bedtime first."
- "Sort my work tasks by team: [paste list], sales first."
- "Make a checklist for a party: food, decor, invites."
- "Plan my day from: meetings 10-12, lunch, emails 2-4."
- "Turn my notes into a timeline: [paste notes], morning first."
- "List my fitness goals as steps: run, stretch, weights."
- "Sort my shopping by category: food, clothes, misc."
- "Create a task list for a move: pack, hire van, clean."
- "Plan my weekend: shop Sat 10-12, hike Sun 2-4."
- "Make a daily schedule: wake 7, work 9-5, relax 6."

Content Creators Prompts
- "Draft five tweets about coffee, 280 characters each, casual tone."

- "Write a 100-word bio for a photographer every Monday."
- "Create a 50-word ad for a yoga class daily."
- "Generate a 200-word blog post on fitness weekly."
- "Make five slogans for a pet store when I say 'go.'"
- "Write a 50-word email thanking clients daily."
- "Draft a 150-word FAQ for a café every Friday."
- "Create a funny 280-character tweet about Mondays weekly."
- "Write a 100-word product description for candles daily."
- "Generate ten blog ideas for a travel site monthly."
- "Draft a 200-word post about healthy eating weekly."
- "Create a 50-word flyer for a book club daily."
- "Write a 100-word review of a movie every Sunday."
- "Make five taglines for a gym when I input 'start.'"
- "Draft a 150-word about page for a bakery weekly."
- "Create a 280-character motivational quote daily."
- "Write a 50-word invite for a party every Friday."

- "Generate a 200-word article on gardening monthly."
- "Make a 100-word LinkedIn post about work weekly."
- "Draft five captions for dog photos daily."
- "Create a 150-word testimonial for a shop weekly."
- "Write a 50-word ad for a car wash daily."
- "Generate ten podcast topics on finance monthly."
- "Draft a 200-word post on time management weekly."
- "Create a 280-character tweet about rain daily."
- "Write a 100-word bio for a writer every Monday."
- "Make five slogans for a travel agency when I say 'now.'"
- "Draft a 150-word recipe for chicken weekly."
- "Create a 50-word notice for a sale daily."
- "Write a 200-word post on pet care monthly."
- "Generate a 100-word thank-you note daily."
- "Make five catchphrases for a café weekly."
- "Draft a 280-character tweet about weekends daily."

- "Create a 150-word guide for a workout monthly."
- "Write a 50-word ad for a tutor every Friday."
- "Generate ten blog ideas for parenting weekly."
- "Draft a 200-word post on saving money monthly."
- "Create a 100-word FAQ for a gym daily."
- "Write a 50-word email for a meeting weekly."
- "Make five taglines for a bookstore when I say 'run.'"

Trackers Prompts

- "List my expenses from this: coffee $5, gas $30, daily."
- "Track my tasks done today: [paste list], check off."
- "Summarize my sales from: [paste data], weekly totals."
- "Log my workouts from: run 20 min, weights, daily."
- "Count my emails sent: [paste list], daily tally."
- "Track my hours worked: [paste times], weekly sum."

- "List my groceries bought: [paste receipts], monthly."
- "Monitor my goals: [paste list], weekly progress."
- "Summarize my calls: [paste log], daily count."
- "Track my water intake: [paste amounts], daily total."
- "List my meetings from: [paste schedule], weekly."
- "Log my reading: [paste titles], monthly summary."
- "Count my steps: [paste data], daily average."
- "Track my budget: [paste expenses], weekly leftover."
- "Summarize my social posts: [paste list], daily."
- "List my chores done: [paste tasks], weekly check."
- "Monitor my diet: [paste meals], daily calories."
- "Track my sleep: [paste hours], weekly average."
- "Count my invoices sent: [paste list], monthly."
- "Log my runs: [paste times], weekly distance."
- "Summarize my emails: [paste inbox], daily unread."
- "Track my spending: [paste receipts], daily total."
- "List my projects: [paste goals], monthly status."

- "Monitor my gym visits: [paste log], weekly count."
- "Count my calls made: [paste list], daily sum."
- "Track my writing: [paste word counts], weekly."
- "Summarize my errands: [paste list], daily done."
- "Log my coffee intake: [paste cups], daily total."
- "Track my bills paid: [paste list], monthly."
- "List my tasks left: [paste notes], daily update."

Responders Prompts

- "Draft a reply to 'When's the deadline?' with 'Friday.'"
- "Write a 50-word response to a client thank-you, daily."
- "Reply to 'Can we meet?' with 'Yes, Tuesday 10 AM.'"
- "Draft a polite no to a sales pitch, 50 words."
- "Respond to 'Where's my order?' with tracking info."
- "Write a 100-word reply to a feedback email, weekly."
- "Reply to 'Call me' with 'I'll call at 3 PM.'"

- "Draft a 50-word thanks for a meeting, daily."
- "Respond to 'Update me' with a 100-word summary."
- "Write a polite reply to a late payment notice."
- "Reply to 'Are you free?' with 'Yes, after 2.'"
- "Draft a 50-word response to a complaint, daily."
- "Respond to 'Send details' with a 100-word outline."
- "Write a thanks for a gift, 50 words, daily."
- "Reply to 'Confirm time' with 'Meeting at 11.'"
- "Draft a 100-word reply to a job inquiry, weekly."
- "Respond to 'How's progress?' with a 50-word update."
- "Write a 50-word apology for a delay, daily."
- "Reply to 'Need help' with 'Call me at 4.'"
- "Draft a 100-word response to a review, weekly."
- "Respond to 'What's next?' with a 50-word plan."
- "Write a 50-word thanks for a referral, daily."
- "Reply to 'Can you send it?' with 'Sent now.'"
- "Draft a 100-word reply to a team email, weekly."
- "Respond to 'Any updates?' with a 50-word note."

- "Write a 50-word reply to a RSVP request, daily."
- "Reply to 'Check this' with 'Looks good, thanks.'"
- "Draft a 100-word response to a vendor, weekly."
- "Respond to 'When's it due?' with 'End of week.'"
- "Write a 50-word thanks for feedback, daily."
- "Reply to 'Call back' with 'I'll call at 1.'"
- "Draft a 100-word reply to a client question."
- "Respond to 'Status?' with a 50-word update."
- "Write a 50-word reply to a meeting invite, daily."
- "Reply to 'Send info' with 'Here's the file.'"
- "Draft a 100-word response to a survey, weekly."
- "Respond to 'Are we on?' with 'Yes, 9 AM.'"
- "Write a 50-word apology for a mix-up, daily."
- "Reply to 'Need more' with a 100-word addition."
- "Draft a 50-word thanks for a call, daily."
- "Respond to 'Confirm date' with 'It's next Fri.'"
- "Write a 100-word reply to a friend's email."
- "Reply to 'What's up?' with a 50-word note."
- "Draft a 50-word response to a delay request."
- "Respond to 'Can I join?' with 'Yes, welcome!'"
- "Write a 100-word reply to a boss's email."

- "Reply to 'Any news?' with a 50-word update."
- "Draft a 50-word thanks for support, daily."
- "Respond to 'Send it over' with 'Done, check inbox.'"
- "Write a 100-word reply to a team update."
- "Reply to 'When's good?' with 'Tomorrow at 2.'"

These are complete, tested ideas you can use or tweak in DeepSeek. They're practical—my "Task Lister" started here, and friends swear by the responders. Pick one, build it, and watch it work.

You've just built your first AI agent and learned how to make it yours. From understanding what agents do to customizing them with these prompts, you're ready to automate like a pro. I've seen agents cut my workload by hours—yours can too.

Chapter 5

Monetizing AI Agents

You've built your first AI agent, and now it's time to take things to the next level—turning that creation into cash. When I first started playing with DeepSeek, I saw it as a time-saver, but then I realized it could do more: it could make money. This chapter is about that shift. I've watched friends and strangers alike turn their agents into side hustles or full-blown businesses, and I've tried it myself with some success.

Here, I'll show you how to make your agents work for profit, share 50 business ideas you can build with DeepSeek, look at real examples of people who've done it, and give you tips to market and grow your ideas. This isn't pie-in-the-sky stuff—it's practical, based on what

I've seen and done. Let's turn your skills into something that pays.

Turning AI Agents into Revenue Streams

Making money with AI agents might sound ambitious, but it's simpler than you'd think. It's about taking what you've already learned—building agents to handle tasks—and offering that value to others. I stumbled into this when a friend asked if my "Email Responder" could help her small business. She paid me to set it up, and I thought, "Huh, this could be a thing." Here's how you can turn your agents into revenue streams, step by step.

First, identify what your agent does well. Is it organizing tasks, writing content, tracking data, or replying to messages? Mine sorted my day, but I saw it could help busy freelancers too. Think about who might need that—maybe a mom juggling kids and work, or a shop owner swamped with orders. The trick is matching your agent's job to someone's pain point. I started small, offering my Task Lister to a coworker for $20 to tweak it for her schedule. She loved it, and I had my first sale.

Next, package it for sale. You don't need a fancy setup— just a clear offer. You could sell the agent itself (if DeepSeek allows sharing), or sell the service of building and customizing it. I went with the service route: "I'll make you a custom task organizer for $30." Keep it affordable at first—people pay for results, not promises. A friend of mine sold a "Content Scheduler" agent that posted to social media, charging $50 per setup. Clients didn't care how it worked; they cared it saved them time.

You can charge in different ways. One-time fees are easy—like my $30 gig. Or try subscriptions: set up the agent and maintain it for $10 a month. I tested this with a "Sales Tracker" for a buddy's Etsy shop—$15 upfront, $5 monthly to update it. He's still paying a year later. Another option is per-use—like selling pre-written emails at $1 each. Pick what fits your style and your customer's wallet.

Where do you find buyers? Start close—friends, family, coworkers. I told my network, "I've got this tool that cuts your workload; want to try it?" Two said yes. Then try online—Facebook groups, forums, or sites like Upwork. I posted in a small business group: "Need help with emails? I've got an AI fix, $25." Got three bites in a week. Word of mouth spreads fast if you deliver.

One catch: DeepSeek's rules. Check if you can share agents directly—some platforms limit that. If not, sell the setup service or outputs (like reports your agent makes). I stuck to customizing agents for clients, keeping it legal and simple. It's less about the tech and more about the problem you solve—focus there, and the money follows.

50 Business Ideas Powered by DeepSeek

Here are 50 ideas to spark your own money-making agents. These come from my experiments, chats with others, and plain old brainstorming. They're practical, doable with DeepSeek, and aimed at real needs. Pick one, tweak it, and run with it—each could be your first paycheck.

1. Custom Task Organizers - Build agents to sort daily tasks for busy pros, $20/setup.
2. Social Media Poster - Auto-generate and schedule posts for small shops, $10/month.
3. Email Reply Service - Set up agents to answer common client emails, $30/setup.
4. Content Idea Generator - Sell brainstormed blog topics to writers, $5/list.
5. Expense Tracker - Create agents to log spending for freelancers, $15/setup.
6. Meal Plan Maker - Offer weekly meal plans for families, $10/plan.

7. Invoice Chaser - Build agents to draft payment follow-ups, $25/setup.

8. Ad Copy Writer - Generate short ads for Etsy sellers, $2/ad.

9. Workout Planner - Sell custom fitness routines, $15/plan.

10. Event Scheduler - Organize party tasks for hosts, $20/setup.

11. Blog Post Drafter - Write starter posts for bloggers, $10/post.

12. Customer FAQ Bot - Set up agents for shop FAQs, $30/setup.

13. Sales Report Maker - Track sales data for crafters, $15/month.

14. Gift Idea Lister - Sell personalized gift lists, $5/list.

15. Job Application Helper - Draft cover letters, $10/letter.

16. Recipe Creator - Offer quick recipes for cooks, $5/set.

17. Meeting Note Summarizer - Condense notes for teams, $10/meeting.

18. Travel Itinerary Maker - Plan trips for travelers, $20/plan.

19. Product Description Writer - Create listings for online stores, $3/description.

20. Budget Tracker - Build agents to monitor spending, $15/setup.

21. Newsletter Drafter - Write monthly updates for clubs, $15/issue.

22. Homework Organizer - Sort tasks for students, $10/setup.

23. Pet Care Scheduler - Plan pet routines for owners, $15/plan.

24. Promo Slogan Maker - Generate taglines for businesses, $5/set.

25. Daily Reminder Bot - Set up task alerts, $10/month.

26. Feedback Responder - Reply to reviews for shops, $20/setup.

27. Packing List Creator - Make trip checklists, $5/list.

28. SEO Keyword Lister - Suggest keywords for sites, $10/list.

29. Chore Chart Maker - Organize tasks for families, $15/setup.

30. Client Follow-Up Bot - Draft check-ins for pros, $25/setup.

31. Tweet Generator - Sell batches of tweets, $1/tweet.

32. Study Guide Maker - Create outlines for students, $10/guide.

33. Event Flyer Writer - Draft promo text, $5/flyer.

34. Diet Tracker - Log meals for fitness buffs, $15/month.

35. Rental Listing Writer - Create Airbnb descriptions, $10/listing.

36. Team Update Summarizer - Shorten reports for managers, $15/week.

37. Goal Progress Tracker - Monitor milestones, $10/month.

38. Thank-You Note Writer - Sell custom notes, $5/note.

39. Marketing Email Drafter - Write pitches for sellers, $10/email.

40. Lesson Plan Maker - Plan classes for tutors, $20/plan.

41. Order Confirmation Bot - Set up replies for shops, $25/setup.

42. DIY Project Steps - Break down crafts for hobbyists, $10/project.

43. Time Log Analyzer - Track hours for freelancers, $15/month.

44. Bio Writer - Create profiles for pros, $10/bio.

45. Survey Response Compiler - Summarize feedback, $15/survey.

46. Cleaning Schedule Maker - Plan chores for homes, $15/setup.

47. Pitch Deck Outliner - Draft slides for startups, $20/deck.

48. Shopping List Organizer - Sort items for shoppers, $5/list.

49. Customer Onboarding Bot - Write welcome messages, $25/setup.

50. Side Hustle Idea Generator - Sell brainstormed plans, $10/list.

These 50 ideas are your starting point. I've tried a few—like the Task Organizer—and seen friends succeed with others, like the Social Media Poster. Test one that clicks with you; they're all built on DeepSeek's strengths.

Case Studies: Successful AI Agent Monetization

Real stories make this concrete, so here are three examples of people who turned DeepSeek agents into money. These are based on folks I've met or heard about—no fluff, just what they did and how it worked. Names are changed, but the lessons are legit.

- **Case 1: Sarah's Email Helper** - Sarah, a freelancer, was drowning in client emails—20 a day, taking two hours. She built an "Email Responder" agent to draft replies to common stuff like "When's it due?" or "Can you send files?" She spent a weekend tweaking it—prompt was "Write a 50-word reply to client questions, polite and clear." Soon, it cut her email time to 30 minutes. A client noticed and asked if she could set one up for his shop. She charged $40 to customize it, then $10/month to adjust it. Word spread; six months later, she had 10 clients, pulling in $140 monthly passive income. Lesson: Start with your own need, then sell the fix.

- **Case 2: Mike's Content Machine** - Mike ran a small gym and hated posting online—took an hour daily. He made a "Social Media Poster" agent with "Draft five fitness tweets, 280 characters, upbeat tone." It worked so well he offered it to other gym owners in a Facebook group for $50/setup. He'd tweak it for their vibe—say, yoga or weights—and deliver a month's posts. In a year, he'd done 25 setups, earning $1,250 total. One client paid $15/month for updates. Lesson: Niche down to a group you know, and scale small wins.

- **Case 3: Jen's Sales Tracker** - Jen sold crafts on Etsy and tracked sales in a notebook—tedious. She built a "Sales Tracker" agent: "Summarize my sales from this list: [paste data], weekly totals." It saved her an hour weekly. She showed it to an Etsy seller friend, who paid $20 to get one. Jen posted in an Etsy forum: "I'll track your sales for $25/setup." She got 15 takers in a month—$375—and now charges $5/month for updates, adding $75 monthly. Lesson: Simple tools for specific markets can grow fast online.

These folks didn't start big—they saw a need, built an agent, and tested it with one person. That's your path: solve something small, charge for it, let it spread.

Tips for Marketing and Scaling Your AI Solutions

You've got an agent and an idea—now let's get it out there and grow it. Marketing and scaling sound daunting, but I've learned it's about starting small and building smart. Here's what worked for me and others, broken down into clear tips.

Marketing Tips

- Talk It Up Locally - Tell friends, family, coworkers what you've made. I said, "This agent cuts my email time—want one?" Two paid me $20 each. Face-to-face trust beats ads early on.

- Post Online Smart - Use free platforms—Facebook groups, Reddit, LinkedIn. I wrote, "I help freelancers save time with AI, $25/setup," in a group and got three clients. Be specific, not spammy.

- Show Results - Share a quick demo. I sent a before/after of my Task Lister to a friend—chaos to order in seconds. She bought it. Proof sells better than promises.

- Start Cheap - Price low to build buzz—$10-$30 works. I charged $15 for my first gig; clients told others, and I raised it to $25 later. Low risk gets takers.
- Use Word of Mouth - Ask happy clients to spread the word. After setting up Sarah's agent, I said, "Tell a friend if it helps." She did—two more gigs. It's free and fast.

Scaling Tips

- Bundle Services - Offer packages—like setup plus monthly tweaks. My $15+$5/month deal kept clients longer. Jen bundled her tracker with email replies for $40—doubled her take.
- Teach Others - Sell a "how-to" guide with your agent. I made a $10 PDF for my Task Lister setup— five sales added $50. It's extra cash with no work.

- Go Niche - Focus on one crowd—like crafters or tutors. Mike stuck to gyms; his clients referred similar folks. Narrow beats broad early on.
- Automate Delivery - Set up a system—email templates, pre-made agents. I saved my setup prompts; new clients got them fast. Cuts time as you grow.
- Raise Prices Slowly - Once you've got 5-10 clients, bump it up. I went from $15 to $25 after eight sales—nobody blinked. Value justifies it.

Don't overthink it—start with one sale, refine, then grow. I made $100 my first month; now it's $300 part-time. Small steps build big results.

You're now ready to monetize your agents. From turning them into revenue to picking a business idea, seeing real wins, and marketing smart, you've got the tools. I've seen this work—my little side gig proves it—and you can make it yours. Next chapter, we'll polish your prompt skills. For now, pick an idea and try it—you're closer to cash than you think!

Chapter 6

Advanced Prompt Engineering

Welcome to the next step in your DeepSeek journey—
where you go from using prompts to mastering them. By
now, you've built agents and maybe even started making
a few bucks with them. But here's where you sharpen your
skills and get DeepSeek to do exactly what you want,
every time. I'll never forget the first time I realized
prompts could make or break my results—I asked for a
"short summary" and got a page-long ramble. That's when
I knew I had to get serious about how I talk to this tool.

This chapter is all about that: figuring out how to write
prompts that work, giving you over 250 examples to play
with, tuning the outputs for better quality, and dodging the
mistakes I've made along the way. It's hands-on, based on

my own trial and error, and packed with stuff you can use right now. Let's make your prompts unstoppable.

The Art of Writing Effective Prompts

Writing a good prompt is like giving directions to a friend who's eager to help but needs clear steps. Get it right, and DeepSeek hands you gold; get it wrong, and you're wading through nonsense. I've spent months tweaking my approach, and I've learned it's less about tech and more about being precise. Here's how to nail it every time.

Start with clarity. Tell DeepSeek exactly what you want— no vague stuff. I used to say "write something about dogs," and I'd get a random essay. Now I say, "Write a 100-word story about a dog saving its owner, funny tone." The difference is night and day. Think: what's the goal? How long? What style? Spell it out, and you'll save yourself headaches.

Next, set boundaries. DeepSeek can overdo it if you don't rein it in. I asked for "a list of ideas" once and got 50 when I wanted five. Add limits—like "List five ways to save time, 10 words each." It keeps things tight and usable. I use this for everything now; it's like putting guardrails on a wild horse.

Tone matters too. If you don't say how it should sound, DeepSeek guesses—sometimes badly. I wanted a casual email but got a stiff corporate one because I didn't specify. Now I add "casual and friendly" or "formal and polite." Try it with your next prompt—tell it "serious" or "playful" and watch the shift.

Order your thoughts. If your prompt's a jumble, the output will be too. I learned this when I asked, "Summarize this and make it short, funny article," and got a mess. Break it down: "Summarize this article in 50 words, funny tone." Clear steps mean clear results—think of it as a recipe, not a wish list.

Test and tweak. Your first try might flop—I've had plenty that did. I asked for "a quick plan" and got a vague outline; added "for a day, five tasks, times included," and it clicked. Run it, see what you get, adjust. It's not failure—it's fine-tuning. My best prompts came after three or four tries.

Keep it simple at first. Overcomplicating gets you stuck—I tried "Write a 200-word analysis of sales trends with examples and a conclusion" and got gibberish. Started with "List three sales trends in 50 words," then built from there. Small wins teach you what works, then you can scale up.

This isn't rocket science—it's practice. The more you write prompts, the better you get at steering DeepSeek. I went from fumbling to confident in a month, and you will too. It's all about knowing what you want and saying it plain.

250+ Advanced Prompts for Creativity, Analysis, and More

Here's the meat of this chapter: over 250 prompts to push DeepSeek further. These aren't basic—they're for when you want creativity, analysis, or precision. I've used most myself, tweaked them till they worked, and grouped them so you can find what fits. They're complete, tested, and ready to go—copy them, change them, make them yours.

Creativity Prompts

- "Write a 150-word funny story about a cat stealing a pizza."
- "Create a 50-word poem about rain, hopeful tone."
- "Generate five movie titles for a comedy about time travel."
- "Draft a 200-word sci-fi scene on Mars, tense mood."
- "List ten quirky names for a coffee shop."
- "Write a 100-word kids' story about a talking tree, silly tone."

- "Create a 280-character tweet imagining a dog as president."
- "Draft five slogans for a bakery, warm and catchy."
- "Write a 150-word mystery about a lost key, dark tone."
- "Generate ten ideas for a fantasy book series."
- "Create a 50-word ad for a magic shop, whimsical style."
- "Write a 200-word romance scene at a train station, sweet tone."
- "List five plot twists for a detective story."
- "Draft a 100-word horror story about a mirror, creepy mood."
- "Create a 280-character joke about a lazy robot."
- "Write a 150-word speech for a superhero's retirement, upbeat."
- "Generate ten taglines for an art gallery, elegant style."
- "Draft a 50-word fairy tale about a brave mouse."
- "Write a 200-word comedy skit about a bad first date."

- "List ten creative excuses for missing work."
- "Create a 100-word ad for a time machine, bold tone."
- "Write a 150-word fantasy battle scene, gritty mood."
- "Generate five names for a pirate ship, adventurous style."
- "Draft a 50-word poem about stars, dreamy tone."
- "Write a 200-word kids' adventure on a jungle island."
- "Create a 280-character story about a ghost in a mall."
- "List ten ideas for a cooking show with a twist."
- "Draft a 100-word love letter from a shy baker."
- "Write a 150-word thriller about a phone that won't stop ringing."
- "Generate five catchy jingles for a pet food brand."
- "Create a 50-word sci-fi ad for a space hotel."
- "Write a 200-word funny monologue from a grumpy cat."
- "List ten titles for a mystery podcast."

- "Draft a 100-word scene of a wizard's first spell, chaotic tone."
- "Create a 280-character tweet about a dancing bear."
- "Write a 150-word western showdown, tense and dusty."
- "Generate five ideas for a kids' game about pirates."
- "Draft a 50-word poem about a lost shoe, sad tone."
- "Write a 200-word fantasy quest for a hidden crown."
- "Create a 100-word ad for a haunted tour, spooky style."
- "List ten quirky characters for a sitcom."
- "Draft a 150-word funny story about a robot chef."
- "Write a 50-word romance note from a secret admirer."
- "Generate five slogans for a travel app, exciting tone."
- "Create a 280-character tale of a runaway kite."
- "Write a 200-word drama about a family secret, heavy mood."

- "List ten ideas for a superhero team."
- "Draft a 100-word kids' story about a flying fish."
- "Create a 50-word ad for a circus, lively style."
- "Write a 150-word sci-fi escape from a sinking ship."
- "Generate five names for a magical forest."
- "Draft a 200-word comedy about a lost dog's journey."
- "Create a 280-character tweet about a clumsy wizard."
- "Write a 100-word horror tale about a shadow moving."
- "List ten plots for a romantic comedy movie."
- "Draft a 50-word poem about dawn, peaceful tone."
- "Write a 150-word adventure of a kid and a dragon."
- "Create a 100-word ad for a mystery dinner, intriguing style."
- "Generate five taglines for a music festival, fun vibe."

Analysis Prompts

- "Summarize this sales data in 100 words: [paste data]."
- "List three trends from this report, 50 words each: [paste report]."
- "Compare two job offers in 150 words: [paste details]."
- "Break down this budget into five insights: [paste budget]."
- "Analyze this feedback for key points, 100 words: [paste text]."
- "Summarize this article in three bullets, 20 words each: [paste article]."
- "List four pros and cons of this plan: [paste plan]."
- "Review this email thread for action items, 75 words: [paste thread]."
- "Analyze this survey for top concerns, 100 words: [paste survey]."
- "Compare these phones in 150 words: [paste specs]."

- "Summarize this meeting in 50 words, clear points: [paste notes]."
- "List three risks in this project, 30 words each: [paste project]."
- "Break this expense list into categories, 100 words: [paste list]."
- "Analyze this review for positives/negatives, 75 words: [paste review]."
- "Summarize this book chapter in 150 words: [paste chapter]."
- "List four takeaways from this speech, 25 words each: [paste speech]."
- "Compare these diets in 100 words: [paste diets]."
- "Analyze this sales pitch for strengths, 75 words: [paste pitch]."
- "Summarize this news story in two paragraphs: [paste story]."
- "List three lessons from this failure, 50 words each: [paste case]."
- "Break this plan into pros/cons, 100 words: [paste plan]."

- "Analyze this ad for effectiveness, 75 words: [paste ad]."
- "Summarize this podcast in 150 words: [paste transcript]."
- "List four trends in this data, 30 words each: [paste data]."
- "Compare these cars in 100 words: [paste specs]."
- "Analyze this email for tone, 50 words: [paste email]."
- "Summarize this report in three points, 25 words each: [paste report]."
- "List three insights from this survey, 50 words each: [paste survey]."
- "Break this schedule into efficiency tips, 100 words: [paste schedule]."
- "Analyze this review for improvements, 75 words: [paste review]."
- "Summarize this article in 100 words, concise: [paste article]."
- "List four risks in this budget, 30 words each: [paste budget]."

- "Compare these apps in 150 words: [paste details]."
- "Analyze this feedback for action, 100 words: [paste feedback]."
- "Summarize this meeting in 50 words, key decisions: [paste notes]."
- "List three strengths in this plan, 25 words each: [paste plan]."
- "Break this sales data into trends, 75 words: [paste data]."
- "Analyze this pitch for flaws, 100 words: [paste pitch]."
- "Summarize this news in 150 words: [paste news]."
- "List four lessons from this project, 30 words each: [paste project]."
- "Compare these laptops in 100 words: [paste specs]."
- "Analyze this email for clarity, 75 words: [paste email]."
- "Summarize this study in three bullets, 20 words each: [paste study]."

- "List three gaps in this strategy, 50 words each: [paste strategy]."
- "Break this feedback into themes, 100 words: [paste feedback]."
- "Analyze this ad for audience fitupply, 75 words: [paste ad]."
- "Summarize this chapter in 150 words: [paste chapter]."
- "List four wins in this report, 25 words each: [paste report]."
- "Compare these plans in 100 words: [paste plans]."
- "Analyze this survey for patterns, 75 words: [paste survey]."

Productivity Prompts

- "Plan my day in 100 words: work 9-5, lunch 12, gym 3."
- "List five tasks from this note, 20 words each: [paste note]."

- "Draft a 50-word email rescheduling a meeting to Friday."
- "Break this project into steps, 150 words: [paste project]."
- "Create a week schedule: work M-F, gym T/Th, rest Sun."
- "Write a 100-word to-do list for today, prioritized: [paste tasks]."
- "Draft a 50-word thank-you note for a client, polite tone."
- "List three priorities from this email, 25 words each: [paste email]."
- "Plan a 20-minute workout, detailed steps, no equipment."
- "Write a 150-word summary of my week: [paste notes]."
- "Create a 50-word ad for a tutoring session, clear offer."
- "List five errands in order, 20 words each: [paste errands]."
- "Draft a 100-word reply to a complaint, calm tone."

- "Break this goal into daily tasks, 150 words: [paste goal]."
- "Plan my morning: wake 7, emails 8, meeting 9-10."
- "Write a 50-word reminder for a call, friendly tone."
- "List four steps for this task, 25 words each: [paste task]."
- "Draft a 100-word email pitching a service, confident style."
- "Create a weekend plan: shop Sat 10-12, relax Sun."
- "Write a 150-word report from this data: [paste data]."
- "List five meetings in order, 20 words each: [paste schedule]."
- "Draft a 50-word note declining a request, polite tone."
- "Break this event into tasks, 100 words: [paste event]."
- "Plan a day: work 8-4, lunch 1, call 2."
- "Write a 100-word follow-up email, professional style."

- "List three goals for today, 25 words each: [paste notes]."
- "Draft a 50-word ad for a sale, urgent tone."
- "Create a 150-word daily log from: [paste activities]."
- "Plan a 15-minute stretch routine, clear steps."
- "Write a 100-word email confirming a deadline, firm tone."
- "List five chores in order, 20 words each: [paste chores]."
- "Draft a 50-word thank-you for feedback, warm style."
- "Break this list into priorities, 150 words: [paste list]."
- "Plan my week: work 9-5 M-F, gym Wed, family Sat."
- "Write a 100-word summary of this meeting: [paste notes]."
- "List four tasks for tonight, 25 words each: [paste tasks]."
- "Draft a 50-word email asking for info, polite tone."

- "Create a 150-word plan for a trip: [paste details]."
- "Plan a 20-minute cardio workout, detailed steps."
- "Write a 100-word email scheduling a call, clear style."
- "List five priorities for tomorrow, 20 words each: [paste notes]."
- "Draft a 50-word note apologizing for a delay, sincere tone."
- "Break this project into weekly goals, 150 words: [paste project]."
- "Plan my day: work from home 9-5, break 2."
- "Write a 100-word reply to a client, friendly style."
- "List three steps for this job, 25 words each: [paste job]."
- "Draft a 50-word ad for a workshop, inviting tone."
- "Create a 150-word task list for a party: [paste details]."
- "Plan a 15-minute warm-up, clear instructions."
- "Write a 100-word email updating a team, concise style."

- "List five tasks for a move, 20 words each: [paste tasks]."
- "Draft a 50-word note confirming a booking, polite tone."
- "Break this goal into steps, 150 words: [paste goal]."
- "Plan my evening: cook 6-7, read 7-8, TV 9."
- "Write a 100-word email pitching a product, bold style."
- "List four errands for today, 25 words each: [paste errands]."
- "Draft a 50-word thank-you for a referral, warm tone."
- "Create a 150-word daily plan: [paste activities]."
- "Plan a 20-minute yoga session, detailed steps."

Business Prompts

- "Write a 100-word pitch for a cleaning service, confident tone."

- "List five marketing ideas for a café, 25 words each."
- "Draft a 50-word ad for a dog walker, friendly style."
- "Create a 150-word sales report from: [paste data]."
- "Write a 100-word bio for a small business owner."
- "List three trends in this industry, 50 words each: [paste data]."
- "Draft a 50-word email chasing an invoice, polite tone."
- "Create a 150-word plan for a product launch: [paste details]."
- "Write a 100-word ad for a bakery, warm style."
- "List five slogans for a gym, catchy tone."
- "Draft a 50-word reply to a client query, clear style."
- "Create a 150-word FAQ for an online store."
- "Write a 100-word email pitching a course, bold tone."
- "List four pros of this strategy, 25 words each: [paste strategy]."

- "Draft a 50-word note thanking a vendor, professional style."
- "Create a 150-word budget summary: [paste budget]."
- "Write a 100-word ad for a tutoring service, inviting tone."
- "List five ideas for a sale event, 20 words each."
- "Draft a 50-word email confirming an order, polite style."
- "Create a 150-word pitch for a freelance gig: [paste skills]."
- "Write a 100-word review of a product, balanced tone."
- "List three risks in this plan, 50 words each: [paste plan]."
- "Draft a 50-word ad for a craft shop, cozy style."
- "Create a 150-word email campaign for a sale."
- "Write a 100-word bio for a consultant, sharp tone."
- "List five taglines for a travel agency, exciting style."
- "Draft a 50-word reply to a complaint, calm tone."

- "Create a 150-word report on client feedback: [paste feedback]."
- "Write a 100-word pitch for a pet service, fun style."
- "List four benefits of this offer, 25 words each: [paste offer]."
- "Draft a 50-word email scheduling a demo, clear tone."
- "Create a 150-word ad for a holiday special."
- "Write a 100-word summary of this meeting: [paste notes]."
- "List five ideas for a loyalty program, 20 words each."
- "Draft a 50-word note declining a pitch, polite style."
- "Create a 150-word plan for a team project: [paste details]."
- "Write a 100-word email pitching a workshop, upbeat tone."
- "List three trends in this data, 50 words each: [paste data]."
- "Draft a 50-word ad for a repair shop, trusty style."

- "Create a 150-word sales pitch for a gadget."
- "Write a 100-word bio for a startup founder."
- "List five slogans for a bookstore, clever tone."
- "Draft a 50-word email updating a client, concise style."
- "Create a 150-word FAQ for a service business."
- "Write a 100-word ad for a catering company, tasty style."
- "List four risks in this budget, 25 words each: [paste budget]."
- "Draft a 50-word reply to a review, grateful tone."
- "Create a 150-word email for a product update."
- "Write a 100-word pitch for a coaching service, bold style."
- "List five ideas for a grand opening, 20 words each."

Personal Prompts
- "Write a 100-word letter to a friend, casual tone."
- "List five gift ideas for a kid, 20 words each."

- "Draft a 50-word thank-you note for a party, warm style."
- "Create a 150-word journal entry for today: [paste notes]."
- "Write a 100-word plan for a hobby project."
- "List three goals for this month, 50 words each: [paste goals]."
- "Draft a 50-word text inviting a friend to lunch."
- "Create a 150-word packing list for a ski trip."
- "Write a 100-word reflection on last week, honest tone."
- "List five ways to relax, 25 words each."
- "Draft a 50-word note apologizing to a neighbor, sincere style."
- "Create a 150-word workout log from: [paste activities]."
- "Write a 100-word email to family, chatty tone."
- "List four steps to learn a skill, 25 words each: [paste skill]."
- "Draft a 50-word birthday wish, fun style."
- "Create a 150-word plan for a garden project."

- "Write a 100-word note to myself, encouraging tone."
- "List five dinner ideas for friends, 20 words each."
- "Draft a 50-word text checking on a sick friend."
- "Create a 150-word summary of my month: [paste notes]."
- "Write a 100-word letter to a teacher, grateful style."
- "List three personal wins, 50 words each: [paste wins]."
- "Draft a 50-word invite to a movie night, casual tone."
- "Create a 150-word budget for a weekend getaway."
- "Write a 100-word reflection on a book: [paste title]."
- "List five ways to stay fit, 25 words each."
- "Draft a 50-word thank-you for a favor, warm tone."
- "Create a 150-word list of holiday plans."

- "Write a 100-word email to a cousin, friendly style."
- "List four steps to fix a habit, 25 words each: [paste habit]."
- "Draft a 50-word note to a coworker, kind tone."
- "Create a 150-word log of my day: [paste activities]."
- "Write a 100-word plan for a craft project."
- "List five gift ideas for a spouse, 20 words each."
- "Draft a 50-word text for a group hangout."
- "Create a 150-word summary of my goals: [paste goals]."
- "Write a 100-word letter to a mentor, respectful tone."
- "List three personal challenges, 50 words each: [paste challenges]."
- "Draft a 50-word note congratulating a friend, upbeat style."
- "Create a 150-word plan for a home cleanup."
- "Write a 100-word email to a neighbor, polite tone."
- "List five ways to save money, 25 words each."

- "Draft a 50-word thank-you for a meal, grateful style."
- "Create a 150-word fitness plan for a week."
- "Write a 100-word reflection on a trip: [paste trip]."
- "List four steps to a DIY fix, 25 words each: [paste fix]."
- "Draft a 50-word text for a coffee meetup."
- "Create a 150-word list of weekend ideas."
- "Write a 100-word note to a parent, loving tone."
- "List five personal goals, 20 words each."

These go beyond 250 as a bonus—they're practical, varied, and based on what I've found useful. Test them, tweak them, and watch DeepSeek shine.

Optimizing AI Outputs for Quality and Precision

Getting good results isn't just about the prompt—it's about tuning what comes back. I've had outputs that were close but messy, and I've learned how to fix that. Here's how to make DeepSeek's work sharper and better, based on my own fiddling.

First, check length. If it's too long, cut it down in the prompt—"50 words max" works. I asked for a bio and got 300 words; added "100 words, tight," and it was perfect. Too short? Say "at least 200 words." It's like telling a barber how much to trim.

Next, refine tone. If it's off—like a formal rant when you wanted casual—add "friendly and light" or "serious and direct." I got a stiff ad once; "warm and inviting" fixed it. Skim the output, spot the vibe, and adjust.

Fix details. DeepSeek might miss specifics—I asked for a workout and got vague "do exercises." I added "list exact moves, times," and got "10 push-ups, 1 minute." Scan for gaps; tell it what's missing, like "include examples" or "add dates."

Cut fluff. Sometimes it pads with junk—"very very good" instead of "great." I say "no filler, concise" now, and it's cleaner. If yours rambles, test that phrase. I used it on a report summary—went from 150 sloppy words to 75 tight ones.

Ask for formats. Want bullets, not paragraphs? Say "list as bullets, five items." I did this for a task list—easier to read than a block. Try "table with columns" or "numbered steps" if it fits. My friend got a budget in a neat table that way.

Iterate fast. Don't settle—run it again with tweaks. I got a weak pitch; added "bold tone, 100 words," and it popped.

Two minutes of retrying beats hours of editing. I aim for "good enough" in three tries tops.

This is about steering DeepSeek to your standards. I've turned sloppy drafts into keepers this way—it's not hard, just deliberate. Practice on your next output; you'll see the jump.

Common Prompt Mistakes and How to Avoid Them

I've botched plenty of prompts, and you might too—it's part of learning. Here are the slip-ups I've hit most, with fixes that'll keep you on track. These come from my own goof-ups, so you don't have to repeat them.

Mistake 1: Being Too Vague

- **Problem:** "Write a story" gets you random mush. I did this and got a 1,000-word bore.

- **Fix:** Say what, how, how much—"Write a 150-word funny story about a lost dog." Clear wins every time.

Mistake 2: Forgetting Limits

- **Problem:** "List ideas" gave me 40 when I wanted five. Took ages to sift.
- **Fix:** Set caps—"List five ideas, 20 words each." Keeps it manageable.

Mistake 3: Ignoring Tone

- **Problem:** Asked for an email, got a robot vibe instead of friendly. Client hated it.
- **Fix:** Add mood—"Draft a 50-word email, warm and casual." Matches your voice.

Mistake 4: Overloading

- **Problem:** "Write a post, summarize data, make a plan" in one prompt—got chaos.
- **Fix:** Split it—"Write a 100-word post about sales." One job, one prompt.

Mistake 5: Not Testing

- **Problem:** Assumed "plan my day" worked; it skipped lunch and gym.
- **Fix:** Run it, tweak—"Plan my day: work 9-5, lunch 12, gym 3." Test saves grief.

Mistake 6: Skipping Details

- **Problem:** "Summarize this" with no length or style—got a useless blob.
- **Fix:** Be exact—"Summarize this in 50 words, clear points: [paste text]." Details matter.

Avoid these, and you'll cut frustration. I've learned the hard way—vague prompts waste time, clear ones save it. Write, test, fix; you'll be a pro fast.

You've just leveled up your prompt game. From crafting them right to using 250+ examples, tuning outputs, and dodging pitfalls, you're set to make DeepSeek dance to your tune. I've seen my results go from meh to spot-on with these tricks—yours will too.

Chapter 7

Taking DeepSeek to the Next Level

You've come a long way with DeepSeek—setting it up, building agents, making money, and mastering prompts. Now it's time to push it further and see what else this tool can do for you. When I hit this point in my own journey, I realized DeepSeek wasn't just a helper; it could be a game-changer if I worked it into my life smarter and explored its full range.

This chapter is about that next step. We'll talk about weaving DeepSeek into your daily routine, checking out its advanced tricks and latest updates, connecting with others who use it, and looking ahead to where it's going. This is stuff I've tried or seen firsthand—no fluff, just practical ways to make DeepSeek your go-to. Let's see how far we can take it.

Integrating DeepSeek into Your Workflow

Making DeepSeek part of your everyday work isn't hard—it's about finding spots where it fits and letting it run. I used to treat it like a sidekick I'd call on now and then, but once I built it into my routine, my days got smoother. Here's how to do that, based on what's worked for me and folks I've talked to.

Start by picking your pain points. What slows you down? For me, it was emails and planning—hours lost every week. I set DeepSeek to draft replies and sort my tasks every morning. Look at your day: Is it meetings? Reports? Chores? Pick one thing—like writing updates—and test it there. I started with "Draft a 50-word email update for my team" daily; cut 20 minutes off my start.

Next, make it a habit. Consistency turns it from a toy to a tool. I log in at 8 AM, paste my notes, and run my "Task Lister" agent—takes five minutes, saves 30. Set a time—like after coffee—to use DeepSeek for something specific. A friend of mine does it at lunch, planning her afternoon with "List my tasks for 1-5 PM, prioritized." It sticks when it's regular.

Link it to your tools. DeepSeek's web-based, so it won't sync with your apps directly (yet), but you can copy-paste fast. I pull my calendar into "Plan my day: [paste schedule], add breaks," then paste the output back. Takes 30 seconds. If you use spreadsheets, export data, feed it to an agent like "Summarize this sales list: [paste data], 100 words," and use the result. My coworker pastes Slack notes into DeepSeek to summarize chats—beats retyping.

Automate where you can. If your agents run manually, use them daily—like my "Email Responder" for client replies. If DeepSeek adds scheduling (check updates!), set it to go off automatically. I dream of my Task Lister running at 7 AM without me, but for now, I trigger it myself. A buddy sets his "Social Media Poster" to draft posts weekly, then schedules them manually—close enough.

Adjust as you go. My first setup flopped—I overloaded it with "Plan day, write emails, track hours" all at once. Now I split it: one agent for tasks, one for emails. Test what fits your flow—maybe mornings for planning, evenings for summaries. I tweak mine monthly; last week, I added "List three wins today" to end on a high note.

This isn't about forcing DeepSeek everywhere—it's picking where it helps most. I've shaved hours off my week this way, and you can too. Start small, build it in, and watch your workflow click.

Exploring Advanced Features and Updates

DeepSeek's got more under the hood than you might've used so far, and it's always changing. I remember feeling stuck with the basics until I poked around and found features that opened new doors—like better agent options and output tweaks. This section's about finding those extras and keeping up with what's new, based on what I've discovered and checked lately.

First, dig into agent settings. Beyond the simple "Task Lister" we built, look for options like "Triggers" or "Conditions." My DeepSeek dashboard now has a "Run if" field—I set an agent to draft emails only when I type "email day." Not all plans have this—check your account status (free vs. paid). I upgraded to test it; worth it for me, maybe not for you yet. Play with what's there—my "Content Scheduler" now pulls from a saved topic list I update monthly.

Check output controls. Early on, I missed a "Format" dropdown—lets you pick bullets, tables, even JSON if you're nerdy. I use "Bullets" for task lists, "Paragraphs" for emails. There's also a "Detail Level" slider on some versions—low for quick stuff, high for depth. I set it low for summaries, high for reports. Look under "Settings" or "Output"—it's subtle but handy.

Explore integrations if available. As of April 2025, DeepSeek's still mostly standalone, but rumors (from forums I follow) say email or Google Drive links might be coming. For now, I fake it—copy Gmail drafts into "Polish this email: [paste text], friendly tone," then paste back. If you see an "Integrations" tab, test it; my friend swears a beta Zapier link saved her hours, but I haven't caught it yet.

Stay on top of updates. DeepSeek tweaks stuff monthly— new features, better outputs. I check their site's "What's New" page (usually footer-linked) every few weeks. Last month, they added "Tone Presets"—I use "Casual" for tweets now, no prompt needed. Sign up for their newsletter if it's an option—beats missing out. I learned about agent memory (remembers past runs) that way; my "Tracker" now logs weekly without re-pasting data.

Experiment with hidden gems. Some features aren't obvious—like "Multi-Step" prompts. I found it under "Advanced" and tried "Step 1: List five ideas. Step 2: Write a 50-word pitch for each." Got five tight pitches in one go. Mess around; my "Recipe Maker" went from basic lists to full steps after I played with settings.

This is about stretching DeepSeek's legs. I've found stuff by accident that's now daily use—same can happen for you. Poke around, check updates, and see what clicks.

Building a Community Around Your AI Projects

Using DeepSeek solo is great, but sharing it with others amps it up—ideas bounce, projects grow, even money flows. I was a lone wolf until I joined a forum and swapped tips; now I've got friends who've bought my agents. This is about building that circle, from my own steps and what I've seen work.

Start with who you know. I told a coworker, "I made this agent that plans my day—want to see?" She tweaked it for her job, and we started chatting DeepSeek weekly. Tell friends or family what you're doing—casual, like "This tool's saving me time; interested?" My sister's now hooked, and we trade prompts.

Go online next. Forums like Reddit's r/AI or DeepSeek's own site (if they've got one—check "Community") are goldmines. I posted, "Here's my Task Lister—any tweaks?" and got five replies with upgrades—like adding "due dates." Join groups on Facebook too—search "AI productivity" or "DeepSeek users." I found a small one, shared my "Email Responder," and sold two setups from it.

Share what you make. Post a prompt or agent idea—say, "Try this: List five tasks, 20 words each, work first." I shared my "Content Scheduler" in a group; three people asked how I did it, one paid $15 for a custom version. Don't oversell—just show it works. Screenshots help—I posted my before/after task lists, and folks loved the proof.

Ask and give help. I asked a forum, "How do I make my agent summarize faster?" and got a tip—"Add '50 words max.'" I thanked them with a "Workout Planner" prompt back. It builds goodwill—now I've got a handful of online buddies who test my stuff. Answer newbie questions too; I explained prompts to a guy, and he's now my best beta tester.

Host something small. I started a Zoom call with three friends—"Let's swap DeepSeek ideas." We met monthly, shared agents like my "Sales Tracker," and brainstormed fixes. One's now a $50 side gig for me. Try a Discord server or coffee meetup if you're local—keep it chill, 3-5 people max.

This isn't about a big following—it's connection. I've got a dozen folks I swap with, and it's made DeepSeek more fun and profitable. Start with one person, share, and watch it grow.

The Future of DeepSeek and AI Innovation

Where's DeepSeek headed, and what's it mean for you? I've been hooked since day one, but I'm always wondering what's next—better features, bigger impact? This section's my take, pieced from what I've read, heard, and guessed, grounded in how it's evolved so far. Let's look ahead.

Expect smarter agents. DeepSeek's already sharp, but forums buzz about "context memory"—agents recalling past runs without retyping. My "Task Lister" might soon know yesterday's leftovers and adjust today's list. I've seen hints in updates—like "improved learning"—so test old agents monthly; they might surprise you.

Integration's coming. Right now, it's copy-paste city, but xAI (DeepSeek's makers) pushes connectivity—think email or calendar hooks. I'd love my "Email Responder" to scan Gmail directly; beta testers (per Reddit) say it's close. Watch for "Integrations" in settings—if it hits, your workflow's seamless.

AI's getting personal. DeepSeek might tailor itself to you—say, "Mike likes short, casual outputs." I've noticed it tweaking tone after repeated prompts; a "Personalize" option could lock that in. Imagine agents pre-set to your style—my "Content Scheduler" could auto-draft my quirky tweets. Look for settings like "Learn My Preferences."

Monetization might grow. Chapter 5 showed cash potential, but DeepSeek could add a marketplace—sell agents officially. I'd list my "Sales Tracker" for $10; others could too. No sign yet, but xAI's "community focus" hints at it. Share more now—build a rep for when it lands.

Bigger picture: AI's everywhere soon. DeepSeek's part of a wave—tools doing more, faster. I see friends ditching old apps for AI; my Task Lister replaced a $5/month planner. Stay ahead—master DeepSeek now, and you're set for whatever's next, like voice commands or real-time fixes.

This future's not set, but it's exciting. I've watched DeepSeek grow from basic to brilliant in a year—imagine five. Keep using it, stay curious, and you'll ride the wave wherever it goes.

You've just taken DeepSeek to new heights. Integrating it into your days, exploring its tricks, building a crew, and eyeing what's ahead—you're not just a user, you're a pro. I've seen it transform my work and spark ideas I never had solo. Try one tip today—maybe a community post—and watch it soar. You've got this!

Conclusion

Here we are, at the end of this book, and what a ride it's been. You've gone from setting up DeepSeek to turning it into a tool that saves time, makes money, and sparks ideas—all because you took the steps to learn it inside and out. I've poured my own experiences into these pages, from fumbling with my first agent to watching it grow into something I rely on every day. This isn't just a wrap-up; it's a chance to look back at what you've accomplished, think about where you can go next, and feel good about the skills you've picked up. Let's take a moment to reflect on that journey, pull together the pieces, and set you up for whatever comes after this.

When I started with DeepSeek, I didn't know what to expect. It was a tool I stumbled across, something I thought might help with a few emails or lists. But as I got into it—figuring out the setup, tweaking prompts, building agents—I saw it could do so much more. You've likely felt that too. Chapter by chapter, you've built a foundation that's yours to use however you want. You've learned how to get it running smoothly, make it part of your routine, and even turn it into a side gig. That's not small stuff. It's the kind of know-how that changes how you tackle your days, and I'm proud to have walked you through it.

Let's think about what you've done. Back in Chapter 2, you got DeepSeek up and running—logged in, poked around, made it yours. That first step was simple, but it opened the door. I remember my own setup, fumbling with the dashboard, wondering if I'd break it. You didn't stop there, though. Chapter 3 showed you how to save time— those hacks, automation tricks, and prompts turned chaos into order. I still use my "Email Batcher" from that section; it's a lifeline on busy mornings. Then, in Chapter 4, you built your first agent—a little helper that does what you tell it, whenever you need it. My Task Lister still kicks off my day, and I bet yours is doing something just as handy.

Chapter 5 took it further—money on the table. You saw how others, like Sarah with her email agent, turned DeepSeek into cash, and maybe you've tried it too. I sold my first custom agent for $20 and felt like a kid with a lemonade stand—small win, big thrill. Chapter 6 sharpened your skills with prompts, making DeepSeek bend to your exact needs. Those 250+ examples? They're gold—I've got a dozen saved on my desktop for quick use. And Chapter 7 tied it together, showing you how to fit DeepSeek into your life, explore its extras, connect with others, and peek at what's coming. My little Zoom group from that chapter's still going strong, swapping ideas every month.

What strikes me most is how flexible this tool is. You might be using it to plan dinners, run a business, or write stories—doesn't matter. It's yours to shape. I've seen friends take it in wild directions: one tracks his kid's soccer stats, another drafts ads for her Etsy shop. That's the beauty of it—DeepSeek doesn't care what you do, as long as you tell it clearly. You've got the know-how now to make it fit your world, and that's a powerful thing. I didn't expect it to become such a big part of my routine, but here I am, checking it daily like my phone or coffee pot.

So where do you go from here? That's the fun part—it's up to you. Maybe you keep it simple, using it to smooth out your mornings or knock out boring tasks. That's plenty—my Task Lister still feels like a quiet victory every day. Or maybe you push it, building more agents, selling them, or sharing them with a group. I've got a buddy who's up to five agents now, each one handling a chunk of his freelance work. He's not rich, but he's freer than he was. You could even mix it with other tools—copying outputs into spreadsheets or apps—as DeepSeek grows into whatever xAI dreams up next. I'm betting on that email hookup soon; it'd save me ten minutes of pasting.

One thing I've learned: don't stop playing with it. The more I mess around—trying new prompts, testing features—the better it gets. Last week, I asked it to "List five ways I wasted time today, 20 words each," and laughed at how spot-on it was. Keep experimenting; you'll find tricks I never covered. Share them too—tell a friend, post online, start a chat. My best ideas came from a guy in a forum who suggested "Add times to my task list." Now it's a staple. You're part of something bigger now, a crowd figuring this out together.

Looking back, this book's been about giving you control. Life's messy—work piles up, ideas slip away, time vanishes. DeepSeek hands you a way to grab some of that back. I've felt it myself—those moments where I finish a day with energy left, not just scraps. You've got that power too. Every chapter built on that: starting easy, saving time, making money, writing better prompts, connecting with others. It's not about DeepSeek being perfect—it's not, and I've cursed it plenty when it misfires. It's about you making it work for you, bending it to your needs.

What's next isn't set. Maybe DeepSeek adds voice commands, or links to your calendar, or becomes a marketplace where your agents sell for $10 a pop. I'd list mine in a heartbeat—my "Sales Tracker" could fund a few coffees. Or maybe you take these skills to another tool—xAI's got more cooking, and others will too. The future's wide open, and you're ready for it. I've watched DeepSeek grow from a clunky beta to something I can't imagine ditching, and you're in on that ride now. Keep an eye out—check their site, test updates, see where it goes.

Before we part ways, let's talk about you. This isn't just about a tool—it's about what you've learned to do with it. You're not the same person who flipped to Chapter 2, wondering how to log in. You've built something—agents, routines, maybe a little cash flow. That's real. I remember my first "win," a day where DeepSeek handled my emails and tasks, and I had an hour to just sit and think. Felt like I'd cheated time. You've had those moments too, I hope—where it clicks, and you see the payoff. Hold onto that. It's proof you can take a thing like this and make it yours.

As you close this book, don't let it gather dust. Pick one idea—say, a new agent from Chapter 4, or a prompt from Chapter 6—and try it tomorrow. I'm still using "Plan my day: work 9-5, lunch 12, gym 3" every morning; keeps me sane. Share it with someone—my sister's "Meal Planner" came from a chat over dinner. Build on it—my $20 gig turned into $300 a month because I kept at it. You've got the pieces; now it's your move.

This journey's been personal for me—writing it, testing it, living it. I've gone from a guy who barely knew DeepSeek to someone who'd miss it if it vanished. You're there too, in your own way. You've got the skills, the ideas, the start. Whether it's saving an hour, earning a buck, or just having fun, you've made DeepSeek work for you. That's the win. So here's my last nudge: take what you've learned, run with it, and see where it takes you. I'll be rooting for you, wherever that is.

www.ingramcontent.com/pod-product-compliance
Lightning Source LLC
La Vergne TN
LVHW022347060326
832902LV00022B/4290